AA

LEISURE GUIDE

Scotland

Authors: Ann F Stonehouse, John Baxter, David Winpenny and Pat and Charles Aithie
Verifier: Ann F Stonehouse
Managing Editor: David Popey
Project Management: Bookwork Creative Associates Ltd
Designers: Liz Baldin of Bookwork and Andrew Milne
Picture Library Manager: Ian Little
Picture Research: Paula Boyd-Barratt and Alice Earle
Cartography provided by the Mapping Services Department of AA Publishing
Copy-editors: Marilynne Lanng of Bookwork and Pamela Stagg
Internal Repro and Image Manipulation: Jacqueline Street
Production: Rachel Davis

Produced by AA Publishing

Reprinted 2007 and 2008
Updated and revised 2010

Published by AA Publishing (a trading name of AA Media Limited, whose registered office is Fanum House, Basing View, Basingstoke, Hampshire RG21 4EA; registered number 06112600).

ISBN 978-0-7495-6693-7 (T)
ISBN 978-0-7495-6706-4 (SS)

A CIP catalogue record for this book is available from the British Library.

Printed and bound in China by C&C

A04393

CONTENTS

RANNOCH MOOR

Welcome to...
Scotland

INTRODUCTION

As the ideal destination for active holidays, the Scottish Highlands were first 'discovered' at the end of the 18th century, when fear of wilderness and mountains gave way to the Romantic movement that celebrated the majesty and wonder of the natural landscape. Visitors came first to gaze in awe, and thrill to major events of recent history that included a doomed Jacobite monarchy and the last gasps of the feudal clan system. By the time Queen Victoria fell in love with it all in the mid-19th century, sporting estates were taking hold, and the country was perceived by some as a limitless playground for the pursuits of hunting, shooting and fishing.

Today, those traditional, monied sports still play an important part in the economy of Scotland, but most visitors are drawn here for other activities – walking, birding and winter-, adventure- and water-sports, including quad-biking, sea-kayaking, mountaineering, white-water rafting and mountain-biking. The opportunities for getting out there and enjoying the landscape are boundless.

In the 20th century, the introduction of major conservation projects encouraged the survival and even the reintroduction of creatures such as otters, red squirrels, ospreys and white-tailed sea eagles, and this work continues into the 21st century with the designation of two national parks, covering the beautiful and accessible Trossachs and Loch Lomond area, and the unique environment of the Cairngorm Mountains.

But as any modern visitor will quickly discover, Scotland is a great deal more than one big adventure playground. There are layers of history to uncover, from prehistoric burial sites and ancient lake dwellings, to castles, battlefields and industrial trails. Scottish hospitality is legendary for its generosity and warmth, and the pleasures of discovering top-class locally produced food such as beef, salmon and seafood, not to mention good whisky, are all part of the essential experience.

In the pages that follow we have included information about what you can see, along with activities to appeal to all, from adrenalin sports to shopping for souvenirs. We've recommended places to eat in each section, from pubs known for their excellent food to grand hotels where afternoon tea is celebrated in style. This book is only the starting point: the real fun is to get out there and discover Scotland for yourself.

Orkney Islands
Thurso
Tongue
Wick
A9
A838
Lewis
The Minch
North West Highlands
Outer Hebrides
Ullapool
Gairloch
SKYE & NORTHERN HIGHLANDS
Tain
8
A832
10
Dingwall
Moray Firth
Fraserburgh
Elgin
Peterhead
9
Portree
Skye
Inverness
2
Grantown-on-Spey
A95
CAIRNGORMS & CENTRAL HIGHLANDS
A90
Kyle of Lochalsh
A82
Inverurie
A87
Aberdeen
7
3
Cairngorms
Mallaig
Kingussie
Braemar
A93
Banchory
6
Fort William
Grampian Mountains
Inner Hebrides
A9
A90
Pitlochry
Montrose
A82
Forfar
TROSSACHS & SOUTHERN HIGHLANDS
Mull
Killin
1
Dundee
Arbroath
Oban
A85
Perth
ARGYLL, MULL & WESTERN HIGHLANDS
3
A9
St Andrews
Inveraray
1
Callander
NORTH SEA
4
Stirling
2
Dunfermline
Firth of Forth
Lochgilphead
Dunbar
Jura
Dunoon
2
Falkirk
A83
5
Greenock
Edinburgh
Livingston
A1
Glasgow
Islay
Kintyre
Peebles
Arran
Kilmarnock
Galashiels
Firth of Clyde
Ayr
M74
A76
A68
Moffat
Cheviot Hills
SOUTHERN SCOTLAND, EDINBURGH & FIFE
A7
A1(M)
1
Dumfries
A77
NORTHERN IRELAND
A69
Stranraer
A75
Kirkcudbright
ENGLAND
A66
M6
A66
Lake District
Middlesbrough
6 Walk start point
1 Cycle start point
2 Tour start point

1

2

3

4

ESSENTIAL SIGHTS

Join the thronging crowds at Edinburgh's fabulous Arts Festival in August...hear the chilling lament of a lone piper at atmospheric Glen Coe...take a cable-car to the top of the Nevis range for stunning panoramic views ... chug nostalgically through the Glenfinnan Valley on the *Jacobite* steam train...slowly navigate the excellent loch system of the Caledonian Canal...play a round of golf on the hallowed links of St Andrews or Turnberry... sail around the islands, steeped in history, off the west coast...follow the intrepid explorer R F Scott's epic journey to Antarctica on the RRS *Discovery*...visit the museums and fine art galleries of cultural Glasgow... don your ski gear and take to the slopes at Aviemore.

5

1 **Ben Nevis & Carn Mor Dearg**
An intrepid skier enjoys unrivalled views of Ben Nevis, Britain's highest mountain at 4,406 feet (1,343m) and Carn Mor Dearg. Climbers usually tackle both peaks at the same time.

2 **Bidean nam Bian**
This is the highest mountain in Argyll (3,765 feet/1,148m) and one of the famous Munros, Scottish peaks over 3,000 feet (900m) high.

3 **Oban Bay**
Evening sunshine bathes Oban in a lovely glow. The port is the start point for ferries to the Inner and Outer Hebrides.

4 **Glenfinnan Viaduct**
The 'Hogwarts Express' was filmed crossing the viaduct in the second Harry Potter film.

5 **Tobermory**
A perfect example of a lovely harbour surrounded by brightly painted houses. Tobermory will be instantly recognisable to millions of children as the setting of the TV series *Balamory*.

6 **Glen Falloch**
The effects of medieval land clearance can be seen here, the land was once covered in the Caledonian Pine Forest.

7 **Glen Affric**
Dog Falls in Glen Affric, a national nature reserve, is popular with walkers. Also, several species of dragonflies breed there.

8 **Eilean Donan Castle**
Visitors to the castle can see most of the rooms which have been restored and are furnished as they were in the 1930s.

9 **Edinburgh**
You can see the Balmoral Hotel from the top of Calton Hill. The hill is topped by an unfinished acropolis, the National Monument.

10 **McManus Gallery, Dundee**
The spiral staircase in the gallery. On view are major paintings, archaeological finds and wildlife displays.

11 **Glasgow**
A Charles Rennie Mackintosh design at House for an Art Lover.

12 **Inveraray Castle Park**
Highland cattle graze in the grounds of this fine castle. Several walks allow you to explore the estate on foot.

6

7

8

9

10

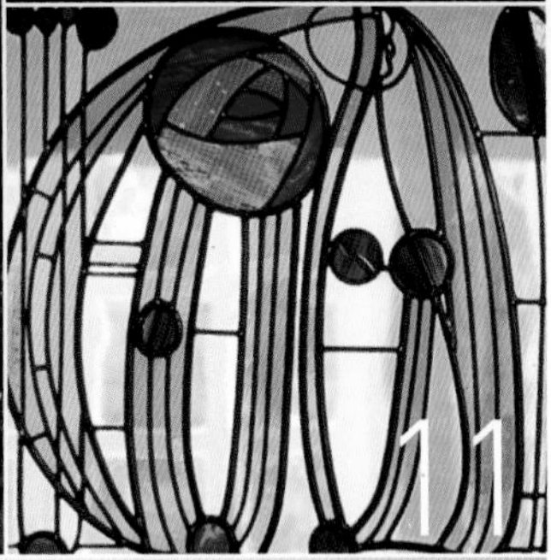
11

12

DAY ONE

For many people a weekend break or a long weekend is a popular way of spending their leisure time. These four pages suggest a loosely planned itinerary designed to ensure that you make the most of your time and see and enjoy the very best the area has to offer. Options for wet weather and children are given where possible.

Friday Night

If your budget will stand it, spend your first night in luxury at The Scotsman, one of Edinburgh's premier hotels, once the headquarters of *The Scotsman* newspaper, and located in the centre of town, close to Waverley Station. Dine in the funky North Bridge Brasserie, or the more formal Vermilion restaurant, before taking a stroll around the city.

Saturday Morning

From the modern Scottish capital, head north across the Forth bridge, passing through the edge of Fife to the ancient capital of Perth. Continue on the fast A9 towards Pitlochry, and turn off to visit the lovely town of Dunkeld. Enjoy a quiet stroll around the 'Little Houses' and the abbey, and perhaps pause for a quick cup of coffee, before returning to the A9. At Ballinluig turn off westwards into the Trossachs on the A827, passing through Aberfeldy and along the northern shore of Loch Tay, under the shadow of Ben Lawers, to the village of Killin.

Saturday Lunch

With several pubs and cafés, this makes a good stop for lunch, and you can walk along to admire the waterfalls by the bridge, called the Falls of Dochart (but mind the traffic).

Saturday Afternoon

Continue west on the A827 and join the A85 as it heads westwards along Glen Dochart until it reaches Crianlarich. Turn south here down Glen Falloch on the A82, which runs parallel for a short distance with the West Highland Way long-distance trail. The routes split once the trail gets beyond Inverarnan. At this point continue down the west shore of Loch Lomond. At Tarbet bear to the right and follow the A83 up over the hill to Arrochar. Follow this route up to the top of the steep pass of Rest and Be Thankful, and enjoy the stunning views back from the car park at the top. Continue around the head of Loch Fyne and treat yourself to a snack at the Loch Fyne Oyster Bar before making your way further on to Inveraray. Cross the old bridge into the town and turn right onto the A819 up Glen Aray. At the top of Loch Awe bear left onto the A85 and follow it into Oban.

Saturday Night

There's a great choice of comfortable B&Bs in Oban – pick one with a view to the island of Kerrera if you can. There are plenty of eating places in this busy little fishing port, or take fresh fish and chips up to McCaig's Folly for a romantic view of the sunset.

REST AND BE THANKFUL PASS, NEAR ARROCHAR

CUILLIN HILLS, SKYE

DAY TWO

Our second and final day starts with a visit to the Sea Life Sanctuary near Barcaldine or a trip to Glen Coe, before driving north through beautiful countryside to Fort William and then on to the 'big scenery' of lochs and mountains and the romantic Eilean Donan. End the weekend on the lovely island of Skye or, alternatively, drive on to the Highland city of Inverness looking out for Scotland's elusive monster of the deep on the way.

Sunday Morning

After a leisurely breakfast, head north on the A85 and turn off to cross the neck of Loch Etive on the Connel Bridge, on the A828. Visit the doe-eyed seals and many other creatures at the Sea Life Sanctuary south of Barcaldine, or go to the loch-divided village of Ballachulish to explore Glen Coe on the A82.

Sunday Lunch

Continue travelling north on the A82 to Fort William, and turn left on the A830 to stop for lunch at the pub by Neptune's Staircase, the lock staircase by Banavie, at the foot of the Caledonian Canal.

Sunday Afternoon and Night

Return to the A82 and turn north, following the road up the Great Glen, along the flank of Loch Lochy. Here you can choose to head west on the A87 towards Skye, or continue northeast to Inverness. If taking the first option, the road leads through dramatic mountains to Loch Duich and the famously picturesque castle of Eilean Donan. You can get a cup of tea and a snack here, before continuing to Kyle of Lochalsh, where the modern road bridge will take you to Skye in the twinkling of an eye. Visit the Brightwater Visitor Centre at Kyleakin village for an insight into the local wildlife, before continuing your exploration of the island. There's plenty of top-notch accommodation and eating places, including the elegant Three Chimneys in the north at Colbost (advance booking is essential).

Alternatively, and for a shorter route, stay on the A82 at Invergarry and you'll soon reach the foot of mysterious Loch Ness. The road runs up the western shore, and at Drumnadrochit you can chase the tall tales of the Loch Ness Monster. The A831 leads off from here towards Cannich and lovely Glen Affric – perfect for a good walk.

Stay on the A82 to reach Inverness, a hub of modern communications and full of hotels and B&Bs. Treat yourself to fine dining amid the ancestral portraits at the Bunchrew House Hotel and spend the night in a luxurious room overlooking Beauly Firth (and keep a watchful eye open for the hotel's ghost as you retire to bed!).

Route facts

MINIMUM TIME The time stated for completing each route is the estimated minimum time that a reasonably fit family group of walkers or cyclists would take to complete the circuit. This does not allow for rest or refreshment stops.

OS MAP Each route is shown on a map. However, some detail is lost because of the restrictions imposed by scale, so for this reason, we recommend that you use the maps in conjunction with a more detailed Ordnance Survey map. The relevant map for each walk or cycle ride is listed.

START This indicates the start location and parking area. This is a six-figure grid reference prefixed by two letters showing which 62.5-mile (100km) square of the National Grid it refers to. You'll find more information on grid references on most Ordnance Survey maps.

CYCLE HIRE We list, within reason, the nearest cycle hire shop/centre.

❶ Here we highlight any potential difficulties or dangers along the cycle ride or walk. If a particular route is suitable for older, fitter children we say so here. Also, we give guidelines of a route's suitability for younger children, for example the symbol 8+ indicates that the route can probably be attempted by children aged 8 years and above.

Walks & Cycle Rides

Each walk and cycle ride has a panel giving information for the walker and cyclist, including the distance, terrain, nature of the paths, and where to park your car.

WALKING

All of the walks are suitable for families, but less experienced family groups, especially those with younger children, should try the shorter walks. Route finding is usually straightforward, but the maps are for guidance only and we recommend that you always take the relevant Ordnance Survey map with you.

Risks

Although each walk has been researched with a view to minimising any risks, no walk in the countryside can be considered to be completely free from risk. Walking in the outdoors will always require a degree of common sense and judgement to ensure that it is as safe as possible, especially for young children.

- Be particularly careful on cliff paths and in upland terrain, where the consequences of a slip can be serious.
- Remember to check tidal conditions before walking on the seashore.
- Some sections of route are by, or cross, busy roads. Remember traffic is a danger even on minor country lanes.
- Be careful around farmyard machinery and livestock.
- Be prepared for the consequences of changes in the weather and check the forecast before you set out.
- Ensure the whole family is properly equipped, wearing suitable clothing and a good pair of boots or sturdy walking shoes. Take waterproof clothing with you and a torch if you are walking in the winter months.
- Remember the weather can change quickly at any time of the year, and in moorland and heathland areas, mist and fog can make route-finding much harder. In summer, take account of the heat and sun by wearing a hat, sunscreen and carrying enough water.
- On walks away from centres of population you should carry a mobile phone, whistle and, if possible, a survival bag. If you do have an accident requiring emergency services, make a note of your position as accurately as possible and dial 999 (or 112 on a mobile).

CYCLING

In devising the cycle rides in this guide, every effort has been made to use designated cycle paths, or to link them with quiet country lanes and waymarked byways and bridleways. In a few cases, some fairly busy B-roads have been used to join up with quieter routes.

Rules of the road

- Ride in single file on narrow and busy roads.
- Be alert, look and listen for traffic, especially on narrow lanes and blind bends and be extra careful when descending steep hills, as loose gravel or a poor road surface can lead to an accident.
- In wet weather make sure that you keep an appropriate distance between you and other riders.
- Make sure you indicate your intentions clearly.
- Brush up on *The Highway Code* before venturing out onto the road.

Off-road safety code of conduct

- Only ride where you know it is legal to do so. Cyclists are not allowed to cycle on on public footpaths (yellow waymarks). The only 'rights of way' open to cyclists are bridleways (blue markers) and unsurfaced tracks, known as byways, which are open to all traffic and waymarked in red.
- Canal tow paths: you need a permit to cycle on some stretches of tow path (www.waterscape.com). Remember that access paths can be steep and slippery so always push your bike under low bridges and by locks.
- Always yield to walkers and horses, giving adequate warning of your approach.
- Don't expect to cycle at high speeds.
- Keep to the main trail to avoid any unnecessary erosion to the area beside the trail and to prevent skidding, especially in wet weather conditions.
- Remember to follow the Country Code.

Preparing your bicycle

Check the wheels, tyres, brakes and cables. Lubricate hubs, pedals, gear mechanisms and cables. Make sure you have a pump, a bell, a rear rack to carry panniers and a set of lights.

Equipment

- A cycling helmet provides essential protection.
- Make sure you are visible to other road users, by wearing light-coloured or luminous clothing in daylight and sashes or reflective strips in failing light and darkness.
- Take extra clothes with you, depending on the season, and a wind/waterproof jacket.
- Carry a basic tool kit, a pump, a strong lock and a first aid kit.
- Always carry enough water for your outing.

Walk Map Legend

	Route		Built-up Area
	Route Waypoint		Woodland Area
	Adjoining Path		Toilet
	Viewpoint	P P	Car Park
	Place of interest		Picnic Area
	Steep Section	START	Cycle Start Point
	Picnic Area		

EDINBURGH CASTLE

Southern Scotland, Edinburgh & Fife

Edinburgh, Scotland's gracious capital city, a rich mix of confident modern style overlaying 18th-century elegance and ancient history, is the gateway for visitors planning to explore the country. Its outstanding museums provide the context for key events and personalities throughout Scottish history, while its thriving arts and commercial scene showcases the best in new Scottish talent. Within easy reach of the city are the miniature delights of Fife and the bustling small towns of the Borders.

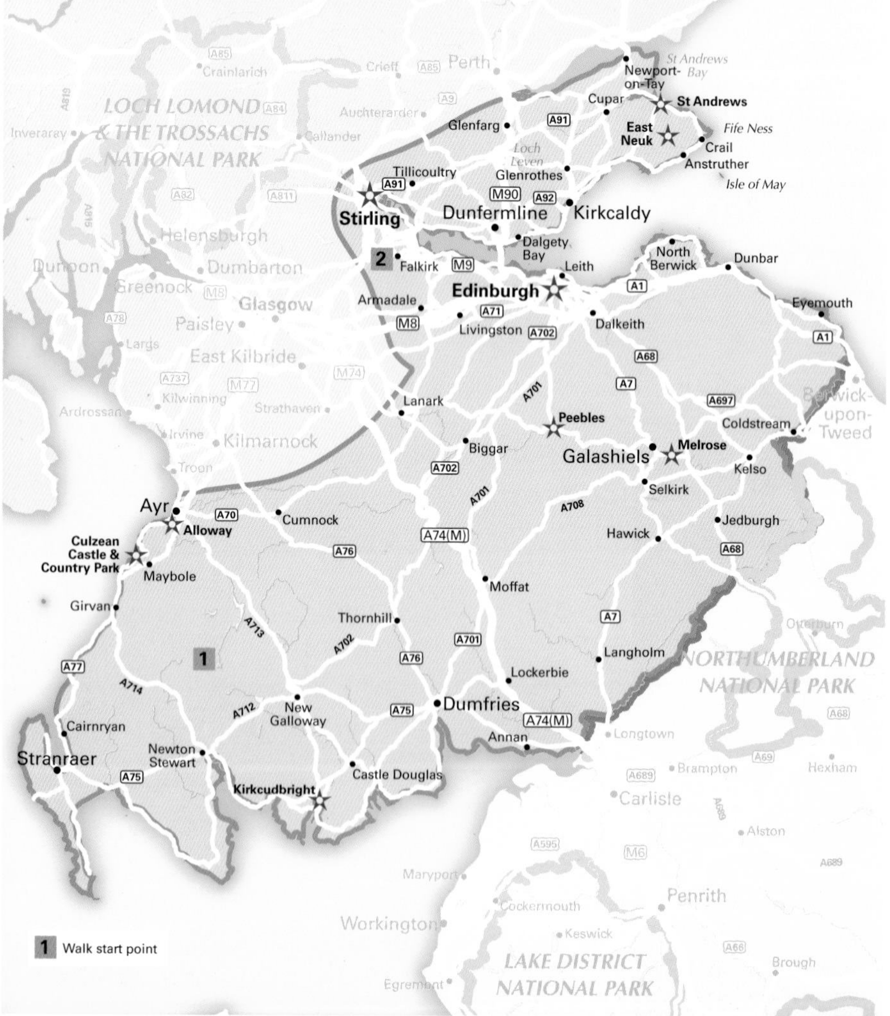

EDINBURGH

EDINBURGH

Unmissable attractions

Skirt the southeastern coastline visiting the picturesque little fishing villages of the East Neuk, with their neat rows of brightly coloured houses and industrious old fishing quays...spend some time in elegant Edinburgh, the jewel of this area's crown, dominated by its magnificent brooding castle high up on a basalt rock hill, and stay to enjoy the world-famous Edinburgh arts festival...don some warm outdoor gear and take to the rugged mass of Arthur's Seat on foot or on a mountain bike...imagine the scenes of carnage at the battlefield of Bannockburn...revel in the eccentricities of famous Scottish authors Robert Burns and Sir Walter Scott...play a leisurely round on one of the hallowed greens at St Andrews or Turnberry.

1

2

3

1 Midlothian Snowsports Centre
Here you can ski or board on the longest artificial slope in Britain.

2 Pittenweem
This traditional fishing village has reinvented itself as a centre for artists.

3 Stirling
The city has stunning Stirling Castle and the Wallace Monument.

4 Arthur's Seat
Edinburgh's residents jog, walk and cycle on this hill near the city centre.

5 St Andrews
A long beach and world-class golf draw visitors here.

6 Edinburgh Festival
Come here in August for the largest arts festival in the world.

Insight

TALE OF DEVOTION
Sweetheart Abbey is a picturesque ruin, overshadowing the little community of New Abbey to the south of Dumfries. It was founded in the 13th century by Dervorgilla, devoted widow of John Balliol. She carried his heart with her in a casket for 20 years, and lies buried with it in the abbey church.

ALLOWAY

MAP REF NS3318

Robert 'Rabbie' Burns (1759–96) is Scotland's most famous poet and songwriter and his birthday (25 January) is celebrated worldwide at haggis suppers. He was born into poverty in a tiny cottage in Alloway. With the new Birthplace Museum and other buildings in the park opposite, this forms the focus of the Burns National Heritage Park.

The Statue House brings to life Burns' famous comic ballad of *Tam O'Shanter*, whose drunken ride home leads him to spy on a party of witches. The Burns Monument, at the far end of the park, is a venue for events, and offers views over Burns' beloved Alloway from its roof. The nearby Auld Brig o'Doon, an elegant stone span, also featured in his poetry.

It is widely recognised that Burns' weaknesses were many. Attempts at farming failed, and his loves and illegitimate children were the stuff of legend – he married Jean Armour in 1788, but only after liaisons with Elizabeth Paton, Mary Campbell and others. Yet his love of life, and celebration of humanity with all its foibles, was extraordinary, and is why his poetry is still enjoyed today. Burns' writings ranged from shrewd and witty observations about everyday life and his beliefs in a universal brotherhood, to the deeply romantic and the downright bawdy. Songs like 'Ae Fond Kiss' and 'Auld Lang Syne' are integral to Scottish culture. Burns' died and is buried in the town of Dumfries.

CULZEAN CASTLE AND COUNTRY PARK

MAP REF NS2310

Culzean, pronounced 'Cullane', is a fine 18th-century mansion perched high above the sea, and it is the National Trust for Scotland's most popular property. That's partly thanks to the surrounding country park – 563 lush green acres (228ha) of wild gardens and leafy woodland riddled with trails. You can discover a walled garden, an aviary, a deer park and lots of follies dotted around.

The golden stone castle, romantically set right at the edge of the cliffs overlooking the island of Ailsa Craig, is handsome rather than beautiful, with its baronial towers and castellated roofline. It is reached via a bridge, and rises high above a terraced garden. Inside, it is an 18th-century show home, the masterpiece of renowned Scottish architect Robert Adam. He worked on it from 1777 to 1792 for the powerful Kennedy family, who had dominated this part of Ayrshire since the 12th century. Highlights include the graceful oval staircase and the Circular Saloon.

The top floor was granted to General Eisenhower in 1945, for his lifetime, as a thanks from the people of Scotland for American help during the Second World War. There are photographs and mementoes of his visit, and for an exclusive thrill, you can even stay the night in the Eisenhower apartment.

EAST NEUK VILLAGES

MAP REF NO5704

A 'fringe of gold' is how James II described the coastal villages of this eastern corner (and 'neuk' is a Scots word for corner) of Fife, way back in the 15th century. However, he was referring to the area's many prosperous little fishing communities rather than golden beaches, although these can be found too, at Elie and around Largo Bay.

Most of this shoreline is rocky, and the villages that cluster around their diminutive harbours seem to be packed in as tightly as sardines huddled against the rising land. They are characterised by neat harbours piled with lobster pots and fishing nets, buildings with pantile roofs and whitewashed, crow step gables, thick stone walls and small windows to fend off the elements – little fisher houses clustered along winding narrow lanes that grew up long before motorised vehicles were dreamed of. In fact, you could drive through Fife on the A917 and overlook these little gems completely, but approach from the sea or on foot along the route of the Fife Coastal Path and it is a different matter.

The East Neuk villages are strung out in line: Elie, St Monans, Pittenweem, Anstruther and Crail. Each has its own character. Picturesque Pittenweem, for instance, was the main fisheries port for the area, and had a priory in the 13th century which was dedicated to Fillan, a 7th-century saint who lived in a cave and converted the local Picts to Christianity.

Anstruther was a major herring port and has the feel of a resort town, with seafront shops selling sweets and fish and chips. It also has a darker side, as an historic centre for smuggling. A chief attraction today is the Scottish Fisheries Museum, an extensive and fascinating collection of fishing craft and stories down the ages. St Monan's, dominated by the squat tower of its 14th-century Auld Kirk, was noted for ship-building as well as fishing in the 19th century.

Elie, with its golden sands, became a popular seaside holiday resort in the 19th century. A causeway leads to a rocky islet, with panoramic views across the Firth of Forth, and a watersports centre. And Crail, the most easterly of the villages, had particularly strong trading links with the Low Countries, which is reflected in its architecture and in the tolbooth bell, which came from Holland in 1520.

EDINBURGH MAP REF NT2473

Edinburgh grew up in medieval times as a warren of narrow streets around the ancient castle. Wealth led to expansion in the 18th century and the gracious development of the New Town.

Today it is the grand home of the new Scottish Parliament, and is the financial, legal and tourism hub of Scotland. Its annual arts festivals are world renowned, and in 2005 the city was declared the first ever literary capital of Europe because of its numerous connections with esteemed writers over the centuries, from Walter Scott, Robert Louis Stevenson and Arthur Conan Doyle to today's writers including children's author, J K Rowling, and Alexander McCall Smith.

Central Edinburgh is relatively compact, and divides into two halves: the narrow, steep, curving streets of the Old Town to the south of Princes Street Gardens, and the neat grid-patterned, broad boulevards and crescents of the New Town to the north of Princes Street.

The Old Town is built along a ridge of rock that stretches from the castle for around a mile eastwards to Holyrood Palace, which lies in the shadow of the tilted volcanic hill of Arthur's Seat. All the main streets run parallel to this line – Queen Street, George Street (great for designer shopping) and Princes Street (good high street shopping) to the north; Castle Street, Lawnmarket, High Street and Canongate (which together form the famous 'Royal Mile') run along the top of the ridge; and Grassmarket, Cowgate and Chambers Street (home to the Royal Museum and Museum of Scotland) less regularly to the south.

The best places to get your bearings are from the top of Calton Hill, at the east end of Princes Street, or standing at the castle esplanade. Views extend north to the Firth of Forth, the Forth bridges and the hills of central Scotland, south to the Pentland Hills, and east to the conical mound of Berwick Law.

The main highlight of the Old Town is magnificent Edinburgh Castle, a solid symbol of the Scottish nation which has withstood centuries of battering. It was mostly destroyed during the Lang Siege of 1567–1573, but was rebuilt by James Douglas, Earl of Morton, regent to the young James VI. Edinburgh's role in modern times as a garrison fortress is celebrated each summer with a military tattoo, with regimental displays and pipe bands from places around the world. The greatest treasures on display here are the royal crown and sceptre, with the Stone of Destiny, on which Scottish kings were once crowned.

The Museum of Scotland is housed in a strikingly modern building in the Old Town. This is where you can see Scottish treasures including the famous Lewis chess pieces, the exquisite 1st-century Hunterston brooch and the beautiful 8th-century Monymusk Reliquary. The comprehensive collections at this fine museum help to explain Scottish history from its earliest times to the present.

Edinburgh's so-called New Town covers an area of about 1 square mile (2.59sq km) to the north of Princes Street, and is characterised by broad streets of spacious terraced houses with

Visit

ROYAL BOTANIC GARDEN
The largest collection of Chinese plants to be found outside China grows in the Royal Botanic Garden in Edinburgh. The Chinese Hillside is just one of the many delights to be explored in this beautiful, green oasis, which has 5,000 plants in the rockery garden alone. The gardens cover 70 acres (28ha) of landscaped and wooded grounds in the north of the city and hide an art gallery, a café and shop.

large windows and ornamental door arches. Until the mid-18th century, Edinburgh had been neatly contained on the ridge between Arthur's Seat and the castle. Conditions became overcrowded and insanitary and, as a new age of scientific advance and intellectual enlightenment dawned, so the need for expansion became clear. A competition was held in 1766 to design a new city to the north. The winner was unknown architect James Craig (1744–1795), and within three years the first house was ready. The first New Town was so successful that a second one was laid out in 1802, extending north towards Leith. While Princes Street has lost its shine in the glare of modern commerce, the broad Charlotte Square, with its fine preserved Georgian House, is the epitome of the planners' intentions.

The North Bridge was needed to enable pedestrians to reach the new city without foundering in the (then) muddy valley. A second link, the Mound, came about by accident, when 'Geordie' Boyd, a clothier in the Old Town, started to dump earth rubble in the marsh. Soon the builders from the New Town joined in, as they dug out foundations for the new buildings and dumped the residue. It took 2 million cartloads of rubble to complete the job, and the causeway became the Mound, later home to the National Gallery. This superb collection of paintings includes works by talented Scottish painters such as Henry Raeburn, Allen Ramsay, David Wilkie and William McTaggart, in addition to international masters including Vermeer, Van Dyke, Raphael and Monet.

Visit

THE ISLE OF MAY

The island is a rocky outcrop in the Firth of Forth, 6 miles (9.7km) offshore and clearly visible from the villages of the East Neuk. It is accessible in summer by boat from Anstruther. Now in the care of Scottish Natural Heritage, it is given over to wildlife, which includes breeding colonies of terns and puffins, eider ducks, and a small resident colony of grey seals. However, there is a long history of human habitation, too, dating back two centuries. St Adrian lived here, until murdered by Vikings in 875. By the 12th century there was a monastery dedicated to him, which has been partially excavated. Today the most significant buildings on the island are the lighthouses, which date to 1636 and 1816 respectively.

Visit

UNDERGROUND EDINBURGH

Edinburgh's Old Town is thickly piled – upon itself. For an atmospheric and rather creepy insight into the living conditions here in the mid-18th century, you can visit Mary King's Close, a narrow alleyway opposite St Giles Cathedral, preserved when the City Chambers were built straight over the top. More of these buried streets riddle the foundations of the Old Town, and can be seen in the Tron Kirk, on the Royal Mile.

Visit

GREYFRIAR'S BOBBY

Edinburgh's favourite statue is much less imposing than the Scott Monument on Princes Street, and stands at the top of Candlemaker Row, opposite the Museum of Scotland. It depicts a Skye terrier, and was raised in 1873 in memory of a little dog who slept faithfully on his master's grave in the nearby Greyfriars Kirkyard for 14 years after the man's death, fed on scraps from local sympathisers.

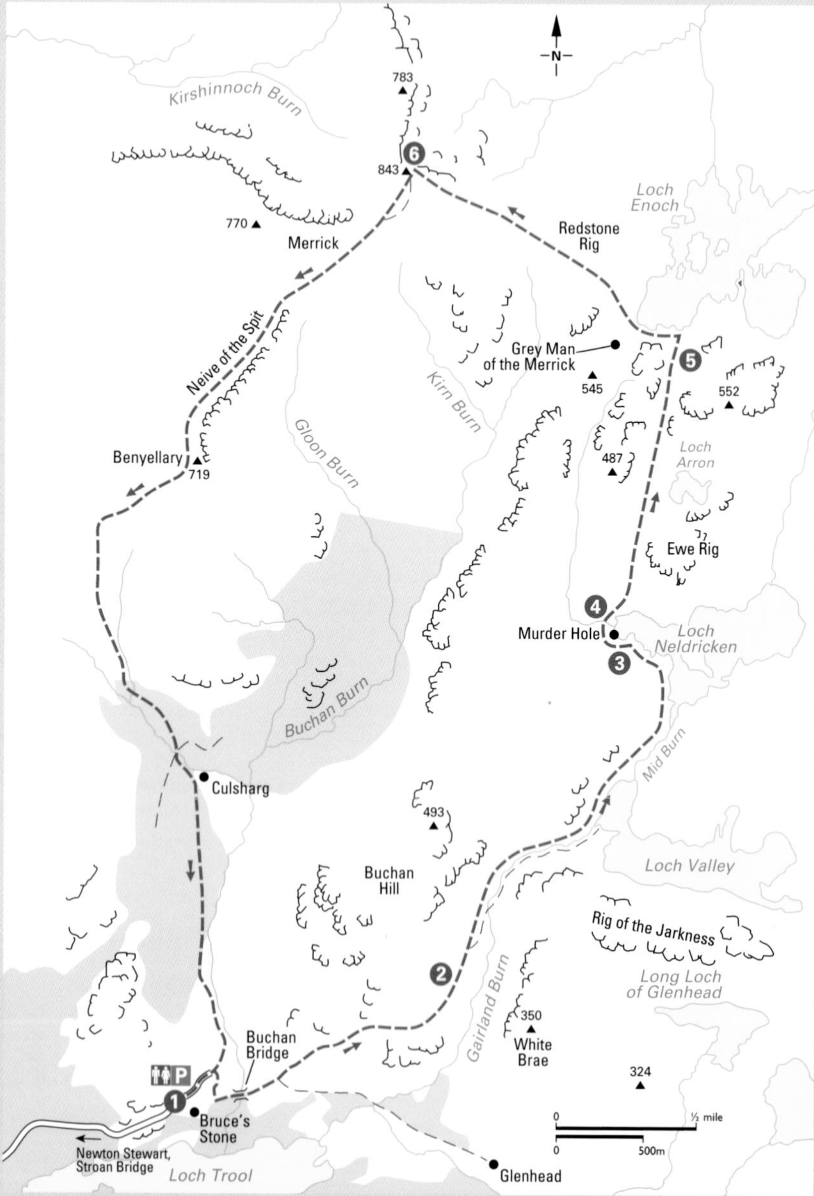
N
783
Kirshinnoch Burn
6
843
770
Merrick
Loch Enoch
Redstone Rig
Neive of the Spit
Grey Man of the Merrick
545
5
552
Kirn Burn
Gloon Burn
Benyellary
719
487
Loch Arron
Ewe Rig
4
Murder Hole
Loch Neldricken
3
Buchan Burn
Mid Burn
Culsharg
493
Loch Valley
Buchan Hill
Rig of the Jarkness
Gairland Burn
Long Loch of Glenhead
2
350
White Brae
Buchan Bridge
324
1
Bruce's Stone
Newton Stewart, Stroan Bridge
Loch Trool
Glenhead
0
½ mile
0
500m

Following the cyclists on the Merrick

A 1940s photograph shows a group of young men gathered round the cairn at the summit of the Merrick, southwest Scotland's highest mountain. Nothing unusual there, except for the fact that they all have bicycles. It's a record of the successful outcome of a challenge from a newspaper editor and a tribute to Davie Bell, one of Ayrshire's cycling pioneers.

Route facts

DISTANCE/TIME 9 miles (14.5km) 5hrs

MAP OS Explorer 318 Galloway Forest North

START Bruce's Stone car park, 3 miles (4.8km) near Newton Stewart; grid reference: NX 415804

TRACKS Hill tracks, section to Loch Enoch can be very boggy, 1 stile

GETTING TO THE START From Newton Stewart, head north on the A714, branch left onto the B7079 and follow it to the car park for Bruce's Stone.

THE PUB The Galloway Arms, 54–58 Victoria Street, Newton Stewart DG8 6DB. Tel: 01671 402653

Route Directions

1 From the car park at Bruce's Stone head east along the narrow road, across the Buchan Bridge. Continue a short distance then turn left and go uphill to cross a stile. Follow the path along the wall, then veer right and head uphill to rejoin the wall. Go through a gate and turn right on to a path. Follow this up the valley of the Gairland Burn with Buchan Hill on your left.

2 To your left is the ridge of Buchan Hill and to the right is White Brae, and to the farside of that the Rig of the Jarkness. Do not cross the Gairland but keep going on the path to reach Loch Valley, skirting it to the west and then continue beside the Mid Burn to reach Loch Neldricken.

3 Head for the far west corner of the loch to find the infamous Murder Hole featured by S R Crockett in his novel *The Raiders* (1894). The story is based on a local legend that unwary travellers were robbed on these hills and their bodies disposed of in the loch.

4 From the Murder Hole head north, first crossing a burn and then a wall. Pass to the west of Ewe Rig and tiny Loch Arron and eventually reach the south side of Loch Enoch. Don't worry if the track vanishes or becomes indistinct, just keep heading north and you'll eventually find yourself at the loch.

5 As you approach Loch Enoch you will see the outline of Mullwarchar beyond it and to the right. When you reach the loch go left and cross another wall. The slope in front of you is the Redstone Rig and although you have 1,000ft (305m) to climb it is not particularly taxing.

6 From the summit cairn of Merrick head downhill towards a narrow ridge called the Neive of the Spit to reach the summit of Benyellary, the Hill of the Eagle. From here follow the footpath downhill beside a dry-stone wall then turn left and keep going downhill, into the forest, to reach the bothy at Culsharg. From there continue downhill to return to the car park at the start.

The tour buses that congregate on Waverley Bridge, by the main railway station, offer the easiest and most efficient introduction to the city, with a choice of four different routes taking in the main attractions and linking you to the sites outside the city centre such as the Botanical Gardens and the old port of Leith. From 2012 trams will also run to Leith.

KIRKCUDBRIGHT

MAP REF NX6851

This pretty harbour town, famous for its artistic associations, lies southwest of Castle Douglas on the road to nowhere, which is perhaps why it has retained so much character. The street plan is medieval, the gap-toothed castle ruin at its heart is 16th century, and its fame as a centre for painters dates from 1901, when artist and 'Glasgow Boy' A E Hornel (1864–1933) settled here, among other artists. Broughton House, on the High Street, where he lived and worked, is now a gallery and museum, with an exquisite Japanese garden. It is said that local residents approached Hornel and his friends for advice whenever their house fronts needed repainting – and this is the explanation for the harmonious shades seen in the High Street today.

More painting by Kirkcudbright artists, including Jessie M King, S J Peploe and Charles Oppenheimer, can be seen in the Tolbooth Art Centre.

Insight box

MARRY IN HASTE...

At one time, under Scottish law, all you had to do to get married was to declare it in front of witnesses – no tedious reading of the banns or familial approval. And so the romantic legend of Gretna Green grew up, as the first village across the border (at least in the west) for runaway lovers from England to tie the knot. Several sites offer a similar service today, and there is still a steady stream of couples eager to start their wedded lives in this otherwise quiet Scottish village.

MELROSE

MAP REF NT5433

This historic town is dominated by its splendid, ruined abbey and its link to Sir Walter Scott (1771–1832), the famous novelist and poet.

The Romans were the first settlers to make an impact here. They built a massive fort, by a bridge over the River Tweed, and called it Trimontium after the three peaks of the Eildon Hills. Learn more at the Three Hills Roman Heritage Centre in the middle of this compact Borders town.

Melrose's more visible history dates from 1136, when David I founded the pink sandstone abbey, which lies just below the town centre. Severely battered by the English in the 14th century, it was later rebuilt, then robbed of its stones by the Douglases, who used them to build a house. Repairs in the 19th century were at the instigation of Sir Walter Scott. The ruins are majestic, and the stone carving outstanding – take time to look upward to identify saints, dragons, flowers, and a pig playing the bagpipes. Look out for the inscription marking the spot where Robert the Bruce's heart lies buried.

Otherwise, it's a genteel town to explore, with delicatessens, an excellent bookshop and Priorwood Garden, dedicated to the art of growing flowers for drying.

Just 2 miles (3.2km) to the west of the town lies Abbotsford, the overblown, turreted grey mansion Scott built for himself in 1812. It is stuffed full of historical curiosities that reflect the eclectic mind of its owner. Some, like the condemned criminals' door from the old Tolbooth in Edinburgh, are built into the very fabric of the house. Others, including treasures such as Rob Roy's purse, an ivory crucifix carried to her death by Mary, Queen of Scots, and a pocket book worked by Flora Macdonald, are displayed in the great man's library and living room, and on the walls of the extraordinary armoury. The overall effect is one of mock, almost theatrical antiquity – a distillation of his novels.

PEEBLES

MAP REF NT2540

The broad main street of this bustling Borders town, 35 miles (56km) south of Edinburgh, always seems busy, its small shops and family businesses doing a brisk trade. Visitors come here to shop and enjoy the feel of a pleasant country town. Walks, trails and cycleways lead into the wooded countryside, starting with the gentle walk upstream from the park along the River Tweed to Neidpath Castle, a 14th-century tower set high above the river (currently closed). You can continue the walk past the castle and return on the opposite bank via a disused railway bridge.

Visit

TEMPLAR SECRETS

The most mysterious building in Scotland is to be found in a quiet mining village, 6 miles (9.7km) south of Edinburgh. It is Rosslyn Chapel, founded in 1446 and part of a major project that foundered. It is linked with the Knights Templar and other secretive societies, and believed by some to be the hiding place of the Holy Grail, a role publicised in Dan Brown's novel *The Da Vinci Code*. Inside is a riot of medieval stone carving. Every part of roof rib, arch, corbel and pillar is encrusted with decorative work – mouldings, foliage and figures of all kinds, including representations of Green Men, the Seven Deadly Sins and other religious themes. Don't miss the famous Prentice Pillar, with its spiralling strands of foliage and winged serpents, necks intertwined, biting their own tails.

Just 6 miles (9.7km) east of the town lies Traquair, the oldest inhabited house in Scotland. An air of romance and ancient secrecy surrounds this beautiful old castle, buried in the trees. Once the Tweed ran so close that the laird could fish from his windows. That changed when the river was re-routed by Sir William Stuart, who also built most of what we see now, in 1566. It started out as a royal hunting lodge at the time of James III – its 'modern' extensions were added way back in 1680, and today it presents a serene, grey-harled face to visitors.

Part of Traquair's sense of mystery comes from its connections with the doomed Stewart cause: Mary, Queen of Scots, stayed here in 1566 (her bed is now in the King's Room), and the famous Bear Gates have not been opened since 1745, when Bonnie Prince Charlie last rode through. There are secret stairs to the hidden Priest's Room, and touching relics of a time when Catholics were persecuted in Scotland. An impressive modern venture has been the revival of a brewery at Traquir. Re-established in 1965, it has proved highly successful – sample the ales in the brewery shop.

Take the winding B712 and B7016 west of Peebles to the bustling little town of Biggar, with a broad main street and wide central square surrounded by local shops and tea rooms. The town's heritage is preserved in a range of interesting museums, well signed from the centre. These include Gladstone Court with its re-creation of an indoor 'street' of shops, and the Greenhill Covenanters' House, linked to religious persecution in the 17th century.

ST ANDREWS & FIFE

MAP REF NO5217

The broad sweeps of golden sands that lie to the north of St Andrews attracted the attention of Adolf Hitler who saw them as the perfect landing site for a planned invasion force during the Second World War. Although his plans came to nothing concrete anti-tank defences may still be glimpsed along the tree line.

The undulating turf between the beaches and the more fertile farmland is known in Scotland as the links, a term which has become almost synonymous with golf courses. St Andrews is where the game is said to have originated, and has six of them, of which the Old Course of the fine Royal and Ancient Golf Club, founded in 1754, is the most famous.

The town itself received its royal charter in the mid-12th century, and the spectacular ruined cathedral above the harbour dates from then. St Andrews retains its medieval street plan, with North Street, South Street and Market Street the main arteries spreading west from the cathedral. Before the building's destruction during the Reformation in the 16th century, this was known as the ecclesiastical heart of Scotland, and a major pilgrimage site.

The castle in its present form dates from around 1390, but was originally constructed by the bishops as essential defence. Its most remarkable features lie underground: the chilling bottle dungeon, 24 feet (7.3m) deep and hewn from solid rock under a tower, from which no prisoner could escape. A mine and counter mine are legacies of an attempt to break a siege of 1546–1547 by the Duke of Argyll. His men tunnelled towards the castle but were thwarted when the defenders dug out a counter-mine and headed them off.

Today, what might have become simply an elegant and sleepy resort town is kept wide awake by its thriving university – Scotland's most venerable – which dates from 1413.

The National Trust for Scotland owns two contrasting properties on this eastern tip of Fife, which both show the hand of the master Arts and Crafts restorer, Robert Lorimer (1864–1929). In the rolling hills to the south of the bustling town of Cupar lies the Hill of Tarvit Mansionhouse, an Edwardian house filled with elegant furniture and fine paintings, and surrounded by formal gardens. In contrast, by a peaceful corner to the south, just inland from St Monans, lies beautiful Kellie Castle, dating from 1360, and restored with eccentric charm by the Lorimer family. The castle is set beside an interesting, rambling, walled Arts and Crafts garden.

STIRLING MAP REF NS8094

This ancient royal burgh grew up around a strategic crossing point of the River Forth before it widens to the east and becomes impassable. The Old Bridge, at the northern end of the town, carried the only route north on this side of the country, and Stirling remained the key to the north until the Kincardine Bridge opened to the southeast in 1936. Plans for a second bridge are under way.

The town's most spectacular landmark is its castle, set high above the once-marshy plain on a rocky crag, and fought over by Scots and English in the 13th and 14th centuries.

It was later remodelled as a royal palace favoured by Stuart kings, becoming the birthplace of James II and James IV, temporary home to an infant Mary, Queen of Scots, and the chosen site of James VI's coronation. Visitors can tour the castle with its re-created kitchens and see the exhibition in the Queen Anne casemates. In the Chapel Royal there are two tapestries that represent a modern reworking of the *Hunt of the Unicorn* series.

Fabulous views from the castle's Esplanade extend to the Campsie Fells in the west and the start of the Highland hills to the north. Several magnificent 17th-century buildings can be seen in the old town, including Argyll's Lodging (once used as a military hospital), before Victorian developments take over at the bottom of the hill.

Stirling's other great landmark is the National Wallace Monument, the tower that crowns Abbey Craig. It was built in a revival of nationalist sentiment in 1869, to commemorate the Battle of Stirling Bridge in 1297, when William Wallace won a victory against Edward I's English forces, killing thousands and hounding the wounded into the marshes to die.

The monument now houses this patriotic hero's broadsword, and you can climb the 246 steps to the top for magnificent views to the distant Forth Bridges.

Just to the south of Stirling, the battlefield of Bannockburn was the site of a major Scots victory in their wars against English oppression in 1314. King Robert the Bruce took on the superior forces of Edward II and won decisively. Stirling was the last English stronghold north of the River Forth, and while its fall was only a stage in the fight for independence (which would continue to rage on for another 14 years), this great victory consolidated the power of King Robert I, effectively silencing any rival claimants to the Scottish throne. For the first time, the Scots were able to present a united front against their old enemy.

Discover a Roman wall and the canal at Falkirk

A stroll along Scotland's old canal system to see the striking 21st-century Falkirk Wheel – the world's first rotating boat lift. It was designed in order to reconnect the Forth and Clyde Canal with the Union Canal, which stretch across the central belt of Scotland, and so restore a centuries-old link between Glasgow and Edinburgh. The visitor centre also has information on the remains of the Roman Antonine Wall.

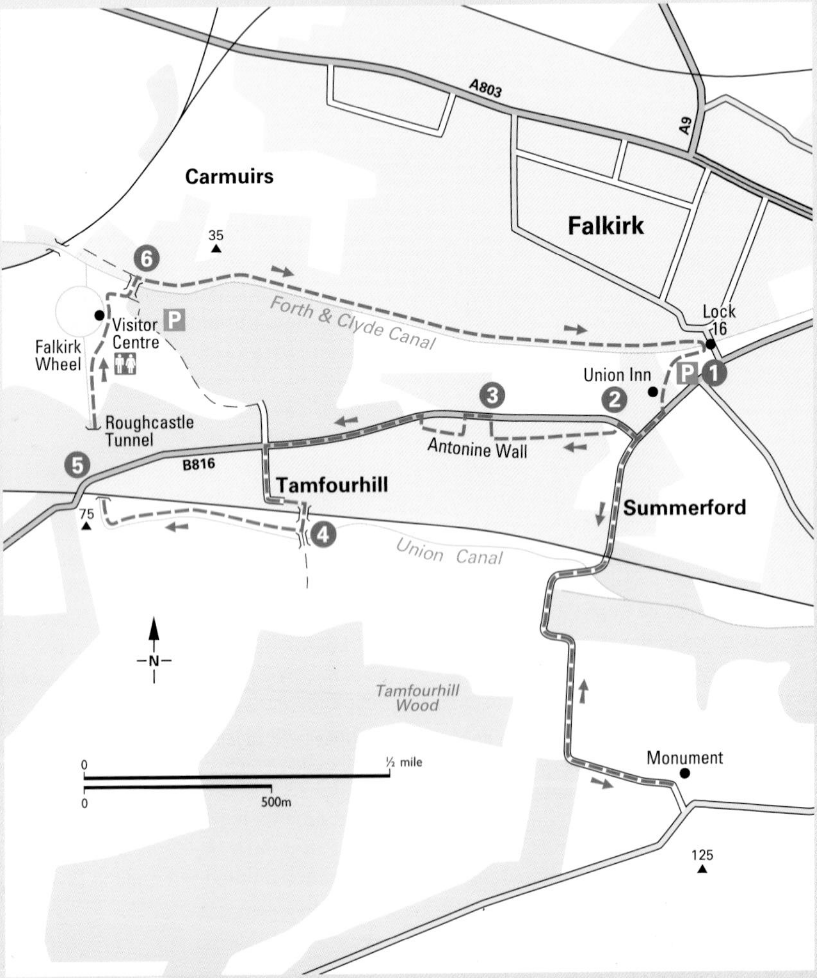

Route Directions

1 Start at the Union Inn by Lock 16. This was once one of the best-known pubs in Scotland and catered for passengers on the canal. Turn right now, away from the canal, then go right along the road. Turn right along Tamfourhill Road and go through the kissing gate on the left-hand side of the road. Alternatively, don't turn up Tamfourhill Road yet, but continue walking uphill to go under the viaduct. Keep walking all the way up until you come to a monument on the left. This commemorates the Battle of Falkirk (1298) in which William Wallace was beaten by Edward I's troops. Retrace your steps, under the viaduct, turn left into Tamfourhill Road, and left through the kissing gate on the left-hand side of the road.

2 This takes you to a section of the Roman Antonine Wall – there's a deep ditch and a rampart behind it. Walk along here, going parallel with Tamfourhill Road. When you reach the point where you can go no further, climb up the bank on the right-hand side and go down the steps to join the road by a kissing gate.

3 Go left to continue along the road – you'll soon see another kissing gate on the left leading you to another, much shorter, section of the wall. Leave the wall, rejoin the road and maintain direction to reach a mini-roundabout. Turn left here, along Maryfield Place. When you reach the end, join the public footpath signed to the canal tow path and woodland walks. Follow this track as it winds up and over the railway bridge, then on to reach the Union Canal.

4 Don't cross the canal but turn right and walk along the tow path. This is a long straight stretch now, popular with local joggers. Eventually you'll reach Roughcastle tunnel – but remember that it currently closes at 6pm to protect the Wheel from the risk of vandalism.

5 Walk through the tunnel – it's bright and clean and dry. This will bring you out to the new Falkirk Wheel (and yet another section of the Antonine Wall). You can walk on as far as the Wheel, then walk down to the visitor centre at the bottom. Bear right from here to cross the little bridge over the Forth and Clyde Canal.

6 Turn right now and walk along the tow path. Lots of dog walkers and cyclists come along here (so take care if you are walking with a dog), while people frequently go canoeing along the canal. Keep walking until you come back to Lock 16, then turn right and cross the canal again to return to the start of the walk at the Union Inn.

Route facts

DISTANCE/TIME 2 miles (3.2km); 4 miles (6.4km) with monument 1h

MAP OS Explorer 349 Falkirk, Cumbernauld & Livingston

START Lock 16, by The Union Inn, grid ref: NS 868800. Falkirk is on the A803

TRACKS Canal tow paths and town streets

GETTING TO THE START
Falkirk lies on the A803 off the M9 motorway, south of Stirling. Take the B816 heading in a southwest direction out of town and after about half a mile (800mm) take a right turn to The Union Inn.

THE PUB The Union Inn, Lock 16, Falkirk. Tel: 01324 613839

PLACES OF INTEREST

Abbotsford
by Melrose.
Tel: 01896 752043;
www.scottsabbotsford.co.uk

Aquarium
The Scores, St Andrews.
Tel: 01334 474786; www.
standrewsaquarium.co.uk

Argyll's Lodging (HS)
Castle Wynd,
Old Town, Stirling.
Tel: 01786 450000

Bannockburn Heritage Centre (NTS)
Glasgow Road, Stirling.
Tel: 01786 812664

Broughton House (NTS)
High Street, Kirkcudbright.
Tel: 0844 493 2246

British Golf Museum
Bruce Embankment,
St Andrews.
Tel: 01334 460046;
www.britishgolfmuseum.co.uk

Burns National Heritage Park (NTS)
Tel: 0844 493 2601;
www.burnsheritagepark.com

Crail Museum and Heritage Centre
62–64 Marketgate, Crail.
Tel: 01333 450869;
www.crailmuseum.org.uk

Culzean Castle and Country Park (NTS)
Maybole, by Ayr.
Tel: 0844 4932149

Edinburgh Castle (HS)
Tel: 0131 225 9846;
www.edinburghcastle.gov.uk

Georgian House
Charlotte Square, Edinburgh.
Tel: 0131 226 3318

Gladstone Court Museum
Biggar.
Tel: 01899 221050; www.
biggarmuseumtrust.co.uk

Greenhill Covenanters' House
Biggar.
Tel: 01899 221050; www.
biggarmuseumtrust.co.uk

Hill of Tarvit Mansionhouse (NTS)
2 miles/3.2km south of Cupar
off A916. Tel: 0844 493 2185

Isle of May/*May Princess*
Kiosk at Anstruther Harbour.
Tel: 01333 310103;
www.isleofmayferry.com

Kellie Castle (NTS)
Northwest of Pittenweem.
Tel: 0844 493 2184

Melrose Abbey (HS)
Melrose. Tel: 01896 822 562

National Gallery of Scotland
The Mound, Edinburgh.
Tel: 0131 624 6200;
www. nationalgalleries.org

National Museum of Scotland
Chambers Steet, Edinburgh.
Tel: 0131 245 7534;
www.nms.ac.uk

National Wallace Monument
Abbey Craig, Stirling.
Tel: 01786 472140;
www.nationalwallace
monument.com

Neidpath Castle
Peebles.
Tel: 01875 870201

Priorwood Garden (NTS)
Melrose.
Tel: 0844 493 2257

The Pineapple
Dunmore Park, Dunmore.
Tel: 01628 825925

Real Mary King's Close
2 Warriston's Close,
High Street, Edinburgh.
Tel: 0845 070 7244; www.
realmarykingsclose.com

Rosslyn Chapel
Roslin.
Tel: 0131 440 2159;
www.rosslynchapel.org

Royal Botanic Garden
Inverleith Row, Edinburgh.
Tel: 0131 552 7171;
www.rbge.org.uk

Scottish Fisheries Museum
Harbourhead, Anstruther.
Tel: 01333 310628;
www.scotfishmuseum.org

St Andrews Cathedral and Castle (HS)
South Street,
St Andrews.
Tel: 01334 477196

Stirling Castle
Upper Castle Hill, Stirling.
Tel: 01786 450000;
www.stirlingcastle.gov.uk

Sweetheart Abbey (HS)
New Abbey.
Tel: 01387 850 397

Three Hills Roman Heritage Centre
The Ormiston,
The Square, Melrose.
Tel: 01896 822651;
www.trimontium.org.uk

Tolbooth Art Centre
High Street, Kirkcudbright.
Tel: 01557 331556;
www.dumfriesmuseum.demon.co.uk

Traquair
Innerleithen.
Tel: 01896 830323;
www.traquair.co.uk

World Famous Old Blacksmith's Shop Visitor Attraction
Gretna Green.
Tel: 01461 338224;
www.gretnagreen.com

■ FOR CHILDREN

Blair Drummond Safari and Adventure Park
Blair Drummond, by Stirling.
Tel: 01786 841456;
www.blairdrummond.com

Cream o'Galloway Visitor Centre
Dairy Co Ltd, Rainton, Gatehouse of Fleet.
Tel: 01557 814040;
www.creamogalloway.co.uk

International Purves Puppets
Puppet Tree House, Broughton Road, Biggar.
Tel: 01899 220631;
www.purvespuppets.com

Old Town Jail
St John Street, Stirling.
Tel: 01786 450050;
www.oldtownjail.com

Red Deer Range
Laggon o'Dee, New Galloway, by Newton Stewart.
Tel: 01671 402420;
www.forestry.gov.uk

Scotland's Secret Bunker
Crown Buildings, Troywood, near St Andrews.
Tel: 01333 310301;
www.secretbunker.co.uk

Scottish Deer Centre
Bow-of-Fife, by Cupar.
Tel:01337 810391;
www.tsdc.co.uk

■ SHOPPING

Harvey Nichols
30–34 St Andrew Square, Edinburgh.
Tel: 0131 524 8388;
www.harveynichols.com

Jenners
48 Princes Street, Edinburgh.
Tel: 0844 800 3725;
www.houseoffraser.co.uk
Edinburgh's most famous department store.

Ocean Terminal
Ocean Drive, Leith, Edinburgh.
Tel: 0131 555 8888;
www.oceanterminal.com
Vast shopping complex.

Gretna Gateway Outlet Village
Glasgow Road, Gretna Green.
Tel: 01461 339028;
www.gretnagateway.com

■ SPORTS & ACTIVITIES

ADVENTURE SPORTS

East Neuk Outdoors
Cellardyke Park, Anstruther.
Tel: 01333 311929

Cluny Clays
Cluny Mains Farm, by Kirkcaldy. Tel: 01592 720374

Active Sports
Chain Bridge Cottage, Annay Road, Melrose.
Tel: 01896 822452;
www.activitiesinscotland.com
Includes cycling, canoeing, archery and motorcycle tours.

COASTAL PATH
Fife Coastal Path. Forth Bridge to Tay Bridge, 81 miles (130km).

CYCLE HIRE

Biketrax
Tollcross, Edinburgh.
Tel: 0131 228 6633

GOLF

Turnberry
Turnberry, Maidens Road, Ayrshire. Tel: 01655 334032;
www.turnberry.co.uk
Three superb courses.

■ EVENTS & CUSTOMS

Edinburgh
Hogmanay, 31 Dec
International Festival and Fringe Festival, Aug
Military Tattoo, Aug
Royal Highland Show held at Ingliston, Jun.

Wigtown
Scottish Book Town Festival, literary festival, Sep.

Selkirk, Hawick, Galashiels
Traditional common ridings, Jun, Jul.

VICTORIA STREET TERRACE, EDINBURGH

Tea Rooms

Clarinda's Tearoom

69 Canongate, Edinburgh EH8 8BS
Tel: 0131 5571888

Frequently marked by a queue outside, this popular tea room/café is conveniently set towards the bottom of Edinburgh's Royal Mile – perfect for a break when you have exhausted yourself visiting Holyrood, Arthur's Seat and the Scottish Parliament. Home-baked cakes, scones and pastries are served from cake stands.

Kind Kyttock's Kitchen

Cross Wynd, Falkland KY15 7BE
Tel: 01337 857477

If you're exploring in Fife, let the aroma of freshly baked scones and pancakes entice you to this well-established tea room in historic Falkland village. The preserves and cakes at the set afternoon tea are home-made, too, and a small selection is offered for sale. Soups, sandwiches and salads are also served at lunchtime.

The Exchange at the Sheraton Grand

1 Festival Square, Edinburgh EH3 9SR. Tel: 0131 2299131; www.sheraton.com

Afternoon tea at this luxurious Edinburgh hotel is a special feature to be relished in the pampered comfort of the Exchange Bar and Lounge. Opt for the simple cream tea, or go the whole hog with delicate finger sandwiches, bridge rolls, scones and teacakes, and an enticing selection of cakes baked by the pastry chef. And if tea seems a bit ordinary, you can choose chilled champagne...

Pubs

Doric Tavern

15–16 Market Street, Edinburgh EH1 1DE
Tel: 0131 225 1084; www.thedoric.co.uk

A good public bar, bistro and wine bar offer something for everybody in this comfortable and authentic popular Old Town hostelry, a short way from the castle. There is a full range of seafood, game, meat and vegetarian dishes on the bistro menu, including Scottish old favourites such as venison and haggis. More traditional pub food is on offer in the Doric Bar.

The Ship Inn

The Toft, Elie KY9 1DT
Tel: 01333 330246

Elie is a perfect place to stop in the East Neuk villages. On the busy waterfront at Elie Bay, The Ship has been here since 1838. Activities such as beach cricket, live music and summer Sunday barbecues all add to the friendly, relaxed atmosphere. The concise menu makes the most of good local suppliers, including fish from St Monans and haggis from nearby Lundin Links. The wide range of beers include Bellhaven Best, and the wine list is extensive and eclectic. Children and dogs are both made welcome here.

Tibbie Shiels Inn

St Mary's Loch TD7 5LH
Tel: 01750 42231; www.tibbieshiels.com

On the isthmus between St Mary's Loch and the Loch of the Lowes, this famous Borders hostelry is named after the woman who first opened it in 1826. Sir Walter Scott and Robert Louis Stevenson are two of its best-known past customers. Meals featuring seasonal vegetables and game can be eaten either in the bar or the dining room, and might include freshly made soup, a venison burger, or tasty fishcakes. Packed lunches are offered if you are planning a day of walking, windsurfing or fishing from here.

LOCH TUMMEL

Trossachs & Southern Highlands

This central belt of Scotland offers superb scenery of hills and mountains, silvery rivers and lochs, with some of the best golf courses in the country. It is a place of dense woodland and fertile farmland, dotted with humble fishing villages and grand mansions, ultra-modern engineering projects and ancient battlefields. Popular with holiday-makers and walkers since the mid-19th century, it has also become the centre of the recent growth of adrenalin sports in Scotland, with opportunities for taking to the water in kayaks, canoes, rafts, and on bodyboards and windsurfers. The more traditional abseiling and hill walking are also popular here.

RIVER TAY, ABERFELDY

TAY BRIDGE, DUNDEE

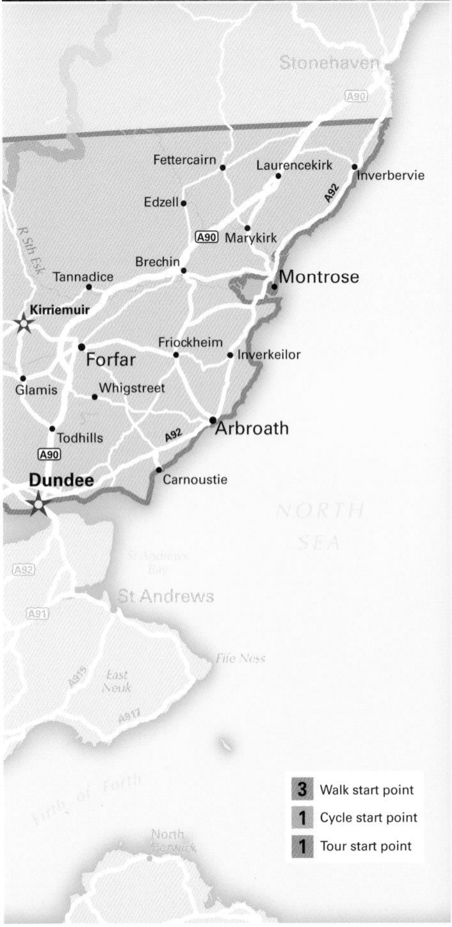

ACHRAY FOREST

Unmissable attractions

Feel the adrenalin rush as you go white-water rafting on the River Tay at Perth...admire the Victorian architecture of Callander, the eastern gateway to the rugged Trossachs...venture below decks on the wooden RRS *Discovery* and see how Captain Scott and his crew lived on their daring exploration to Antarctica...sample the best of Scottish whisky at one of the area's many distilleries...visit the Scottish Crannog Centre where you can see restored Iron Age dwellings and craftsmen demonstrating crafts of days gone by...witness magnificent ospreys in the nest or circling high above near Dunkeld...enjoy the breathtaking view of the dramatic and beautiful Glen Lyon.

1

2

3

1 Edzell Castle
The castle is partly in ruins, but enough remains for an enjoyable visit, and its summer house is intact. The real glory here is the walled garden, which was re-created in the 1930s.

2 The Knock, Crieff
The town of Crieff sits on Knock Hill, although the summit is outside the town. The views across the countryside are simply magnificent.

3 The Hermitage, Dunkeld
This is a grove of giant trees by the rapids and waterfalls of the River Braan in Perthshire.

4 RRS *Discovery*
Robert Falcon Scott's successful Royal Navy career saw him promoted to the rank of Commander in the same month he became leader of an Antarctic expedition aboard *Discovery*. Scott wrote about the 1901–1904 journey in the book *The Voyage of the Discovery*, published in 1905. The vessel is now moored in Dundee.

5 Cycling near Crieff
Cycling in Perthshire is as popular as ever, with challenging routes through the hilly country.

6 Aberfeldy
Canoeing on a quiet stretch of water at Loch Tay near Aberfeldy. White-water rafting is another popular activity in the area along with waterskiing.

ABERFELDY MAP REF NN8649

Born in Ireland, General George Wade (1673–1748) served as Commander-in-Chief of North Britain from 1724 to 1740, and left his long-lasting mark on the Scottish Highlands in the form of almost 250 miles (400km) of military roads and some 40 bridges to go with them. Today, one of his finest bridges still carries the traffic of the A827 over the River Tay at Aberfeldy, a pleasant stone-built town in the heart of Perthshire. The bridge's elegant structure, with its four obelisks and five graceful spans, was designed for Wade by the architect William Adam. On the bank near by stands a monument to the Black Watch Regiment.

Signs in the town point the way to walking trails that lead to the Birks of Aberfeldy, birchwoods celebrated by the poet Robert Burns. The town's historic watermill is now the setting for an excellent bookshop, gallery, music shop and café. On the edge of the town, the Dewar's distillery offers a visitor centre and tour, culminating in a tasting. Outside you might see native red squirrels. To the west, at Weem, is the 16th-century stronghold of Castle Menzies, a restored Z-plan tower house. One of the rooms used by Bonnie Prince Charlie has been furnished and decorated in a style he would know.

Loch Tay lies 5 miles (8km) to the west of Aberfeldy, with the picturesque village of Kenmore at its eastern end. A splendidly spired gateway marks an entrance to privately owned Taymouth Castle. The town also has a great watersports centre, but its most unusual attraction is a replica round-house or crannog, set low over the waters of the loch.

This is part of the Scottish Crannog Centre, the visitor centre for an on-going project that is exploring and excavating the 18 or so similar Iron Age dwellings that once lined these shores. Crannogs were community dwellings built on wooden stilts. The cold, peaty water of the loch has helped to preserve timber, plant and food remains and even scraps of cloth, and the discoveries made here reveal much about the way of life of the crannog builders. Visitors are able to watch demonstrations of ancient crafts and to participate in them.

Shortly before it reaches Aberfeldy, the Tay is joined by the waters of the River Lyon. This river flows down from one of Scotland's most beautiful valleys, Glen Lyon, which lies sandwiched between Loch Tay and Loch Rannoch. Entry to the glen is via the dramatic, steep-sided pass at Fortingall, or over the mountain pass by Ben Lawers.

Insight

PONTIUS PILATE

The pretty hamlet of Fortingall, at the entrance to Glen Lyon, is claimed by some to be the birthplace of Pontius Pilate. It is said that he was born here, the son of a Roman soldier and a local girl, before rising to become the Roman prefect of Judea and Samaria. His most notorious act was to condemn Christ to crucifixion, and tales of his ultimate fate are obscure – did he really convert to Christianity and live to a ripe old age in Switzerland? The Fortingall connection seems to have arisen from a mysterious headstone in the churchyard, marked simply 'PP'.

CALLANDER MAP REF NN6307

Callander straddles the A84 northwest of Stirling, and is the eastern gateway to the Trossachs. During the 19th century it was a flourishing resort town, and the grandeur of the Victorian buildings along its main street bears this out.

On a summer's day the little town is packed out with visitors, keen to enjoy the varied shops and tea rooms, and to track down the history of Rob Roy, a folk hero. Rob Roy MacGregor (1671–1734) took refuge with his people in the local hills, and his story is told at the visitor centre in the former church on the main square. His grave is in the churchyard at Balquhidder. There are several good walks from the town centre, leading to Bracklinn Falls and the Callander Crags.

The Hamilton Toy Collection in Main Street has toys from the 19th century onwards, including dolls, teddy bears, model train sets, toy soldiers, books, jigsaws and games. It is as popular with adults eager to relive their childhood days, as with children.

To the west of the town, beyond the woollen weaving mill and display at Kilmahog, is the scenic spot of the Pass of Leny, with the Falls of Leny accessible from the roadside car park. Of interest to cycling enthusiasts, the Callander to Strathyre Cycleway runs past here too, following the route of the former railway line from Callander up the western shore of Loch Lubnaig towards Killin.

To the southwest of Callander lies the Lake of Menteith, where you can hire a boat and fishing tackle and try casting for rainbow trout. Alternatively, a ferry goes out to the lovely tree-covered island where the romantic ruins of Inchmahome Priory stand. Augustinian monks made it their home in 1238, and the infant Mary, Queen of Scots was hidden here for three weeks in 1547 after the Battle of Pinkie Cleugh before she was smuggled to safety in France.

Southeast of Callander on the A84 lies the rural village of Doune, with a substantial ruined castle at its heart, hidden amid the trees on a curve of the River Teith. Built by the powerful regent of Scotland, Robert Stewart, Duke of Albany, in the late 14th century, it is comparatively simple in construction, with a main block of buildings set within a courtyard and contained by a mighty curtain wall. The fabric of the castle is maintained by Historic Scotland. You can climb to the top of this for panoramic views of the village and the surrounding countryside, and there are lots of little stairways and chambers to explore. Its medieval austerity and imposing stature gave the castle a starring role in the film *Monty Python and the Holy Grail*.

Insight

WHO PAYS THE FERRYMAN?

Until 1535, anybody wishing to cross the River Teith at Doune had to pay a ferryman to be rowed across. One day James Spittal was refused passage when he showed up without any money. Spittal was the wealthy tailor to James IV, and took the slight personally. It is said that, out of spiteful anger, he paid for the building of a bridge here to permanently deprive the ferryman of his living. The bridge is still standing, though it was modified in 1866.

Above Callander

Steep wooded paths lead you through the crags for superb views of the Trossachs. As you climb through the trees and scramble over the rocks above Callander, it is easy to imagine yourself back in the late 17th century, when Rob Roy, one of the most colourful characters in Scottish history, and his loyal band of clansmen lived as outlaws in the heart of the Trossachs. Known unofficially as the eastern gateway to the Highlands, Callander is a great place to strike out from and explore the breath-taking surrounding countryside with its snow-clad mountain backdrop.

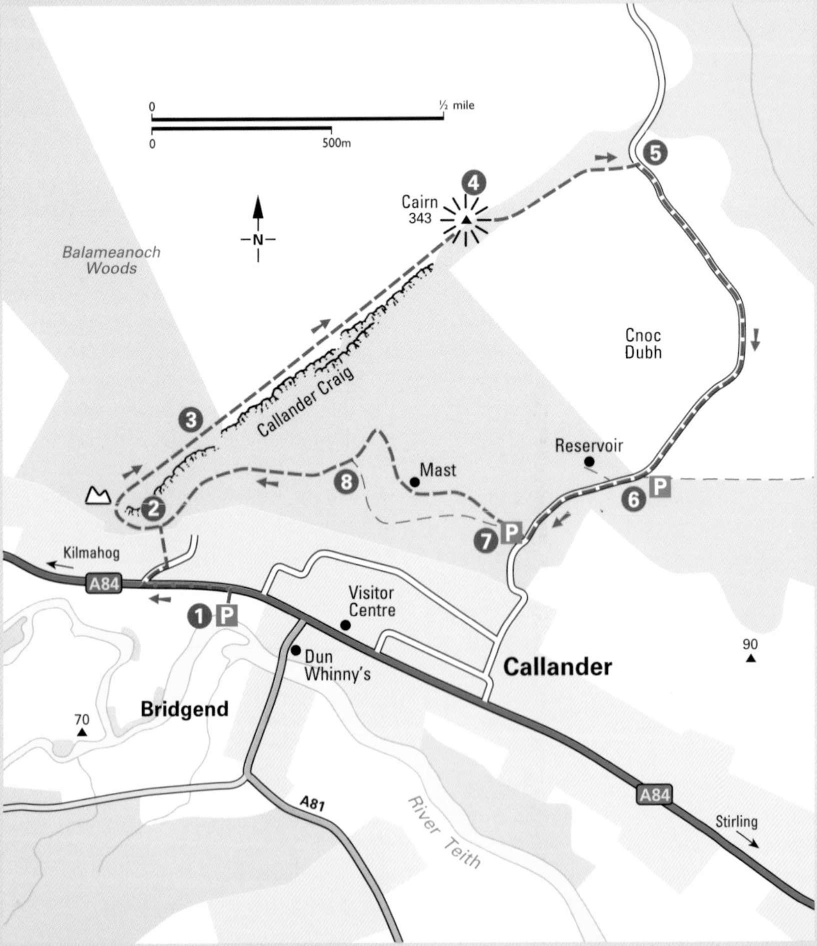

Route Directions

1 From the Riverside car park, walk back to the main road, then turn left. Follow this, then turn right along Tulipan Crescent. Just in front of some modern flats, turn left and follow the wide track. Where the track splits, take the path on the left that is signposted 'The Crags'.

2 Your path now winds steeply uphill through the trees and can get slippery if there's been a lot of rain. Keep following the path and cross a footbridge. Climb to reach a wall on the left-hand side, after which your path narrows. Follow along it to pass a large boulder.

3 Continue following the path, which eventually bears left, up some steps to a fence. Cross another footbridge, scramble over some rocks and go through a metal kissing gate. You eventually come to a memorial cairn, created in 1897 for Queen Victoria's Diamond Jubilee. On a clear day there are stunning, panoramic views of the surrounding countryside from here.

4 Leaving the cairn, your path now begins to wind downhill. It's rocky in places and you'll need to take some care as you descend. Follow the path down to the road.

5 Turn right along the road – you'll see the Wallace Monument near Stirling in the far distance. You'll soon pass a sign on the right-hand side for the Red Well, where the water runs a distinctly reddish colour owing to the presence of iron traces in the local rock. Continue until you reach a car park on your left. You can make a detour here to see the Bracklyn Falls.

6 After the car park, stay on the road for about 0.25 mile (400m) passing a track up to a reservoir on your right, then turn right into the Forestry Commission car park (signposted 'The Crags').

7 Continue to walk through a car park on to a broad Forestry Commission track. Continue walking past the telecommunications mast. At the end of the track, turn left and then walk downhill until you reach a wooden seat and a footbridge.

8 Take the path that runs to the right of the seat (don't cross the footbridge). Follow the path as it runs downhill and takes you back to the place at which you entered the woods. Turn right, then go left along the main road and walk back into Callander to the car park at the start of the walk.

Route facts

DISTANCE/TIME 4 miles (6.4km) 2h15

MAP OS Explorer 365 The Trossachs

START Riverside car park, grid ref: NN 625079

TRACKS Forest tracks and some rocky paths

GETTING TO THE START
From Stirling take the A84 northwest for 13 miles (21km), entering Callander. The Riverside car park is situated on the left-hand side of the road, shortly after passing the Visitor Centre on the right.

THE PUB The Lade Inn, Kilmahog, just west of Callander.
Tel: 01877 330152

CRIEFF MAP REF NN8722

The old spa town of Crieff lies above the River Earn west of Perth, on the edge of the Highlands. For a time in the 17th century it took the alternative name of Drummond, in honour of local patrons, but the original name was restored in the 18th century, after the town was burned down by Jacobite rebels.

Crieff grew up as a centre for cattle drovers, who passed through here on their way south to England or north to the Highlands. The linen and tanning industries thrived for a while, but were overtaken by the growth of the Lowland factories. Today Crieff is an industrious service town, celebrated for the quality of its schools, and as a main hub for activities including fishing, cycling, and water sports on Loch Earn. There is good walking through the hills, too, with a signposted trail from the town centre north to Knock Hill offering great views.

The Drummonds had their castle 3 miles (4.8km) south of the town, and while the castle itself is still private, the fabulous formal 17th-century garden has been restored to its former state and is open on summer afternoons. The burial chapel of the Drummonds stands beside the Innerpeffray Library, founded in 1691 and remarkable as the oldest lending library in Scotland.

To the north of Crieff a narrow road leads up the remote Glen Turret to Loch Turret, passing the scenic beauty spot at the waterfalls of the same name. Begun in 1775, Glenturret Distillery is home to the Famous Grouse Experience, which is entertaining and offers a glimpse into the serious business of making whisky.

DUNDEE MAP REF NO4030

Dundee was founded on a 19th-century industrial base which was famously reduced to the three 'J's: jam, jute and journalism. Today it is busy reinventing itself as a lively centre for the arts and hands-on science, and celebrating its maritime and industrial heritage. The main focus of rejuvenation has been along the waterfront, where the three-masted Royal Research Ship *Discovery* is now berthed. She was built here in 1900–1901, using expertise developed for the whaling industry, and her maiden voyage was to the Antarctic. In 1902 she became trapped in the pack ice, and survived two timber-crunching winters before breaking free and sailing home. The modern museum alongside tells her story. Nothing beats exploring the ship herself, however, and seeing the cramped conditions of the brave men who crewed her for years at a time.

Moored near by, the frigate *Unicorn* was built in 1824 and is the oldest British warship afloat. In the same corner is Sensation, a state-of-the-art celebration of science geared to children, centred on the five senses.

Wool and flax were both woven in Dundee, long before the advent of jute in the early 19th century caused a boom in the town's growth. The plant fibre was imported from India and softened with whale oil before being spun and woven. By the 1870s most Indian mills were undercutting Dundee prices, and the industry had to scale down. It was hit hard again by the post-First World War recession. A fascinating survivor is the Verdant Works, which explains among other things how Dundee developed so quickly, and why more women than men were employed by the jute industry.

D C Thomson (1861–1964), son of a Dundee shipping entrepreneur, founded the newspaper company that still bears his name in 1906. The *Sunday Post* and the *Weekly News* are still produced here, along with many local papers, but the company's best loved creations were its popular comics for children, the *Beano* and *Dandy*. Statues of the characters Minnie the Minx and Desperate Dan can be seen on the High Street.

DUNKELD MAP REF NO0243

A picturesque little 18th-century town with a tiny Gothic cathedral, Dunkeld lies surrounded by glorious woodland on the banks of the River Tay. Everything here, bar the cathedral, was destroyed by the Jacobites after their 1689 victory at Killiecrankie. When it was rebuilt, terraced cottages were squeezed into a compact centre of just two main streets: Cathedral Street and High Street, with a neat little square, called The Cross. The pleasing uniformity of Dunkeld owes much to this rebuilding by the Dukes of Atholl, and more to the carefully done restoration of around 20 houses by the National Trust for Scotland since the 1950s. The Trust has a shop in the main square, in a building distinctive for the iron 'ell' mounted on its exterior. The ell was a unit of measurement equivalent to 37 inches (94cm). The graceful stone bridge which links Dunkeld to Inver, much favoured as a subject by painters, was a masterpiece in 1809 of the great engineer Thomas Telford.

Insight

SHAKEY TOUN

To the west of Crieff on the A85, the small peaceful town of Comrie has a secret. It was built directly over the geological fault of the Highland Boundary, and in the 19th century it was known as the earthquake capital of Scotland. Seismologists in the 1830s recorded more than 7,000 tremors, along with strange loud noises and sulphurous smells. No serious damage was reported. As a legacy of this activity, Earthquake House stands to the west of the town. It was originally built as a recording station in 1869. Its interior, restored in the 1980s and with modern equipment set up alongside the original seismographs, may be viewed through the single display window.

Insight

THE WORST POET IN THE WORLD

Self-taught poet William McGonagall (1830–1902) retains a special place in Scottish hearts for his notoriously bad verse. A Dundee handloom weaver, McGonagal published his first poetry collection in 1878, to the acclaim of many Edinburgh students. His heartfelt verses on the Tay Bridge disaster of 1879, when the bridge collapsed under a passenger train, are particularly memorable for their naïve sentiment and lack of poetic rhythm.

Visit

OSPREY HAVEN

The Loch of the Lowes lies to the east of Dunkeld, and is noted for its breeding ospreys. These mighty birds of prey migrate to this spot from west Africa towards the end of March, and have successfully bred here since 1970. Watch them on the nest, and enjoy the rest of the birdlife from the visitor centre, operated by the Scottish Wildlife Trust.

Dunkeld's ruined cathedral stands in a picturesque, shady setting on the banks of the river, and the crumbled building dates back to the 13th century, although its history as a monastic site goes back to the 6th century. Kenneth MacAlpin, the first king of Scotland, brought St Columba's bones here from Iona in around 850, thereby making it an important medieval ecclesiastical centre. The most substantial part left standing today is the choir, which still serves as the parish church. Close by the end of the cathedral furthest from the main entrance, look out for a sign indicating the 'Parent Larch'. This particular tree was imported from Austria in 1738, and became the source of many trees in and around nearby forests, planted up by the Dukes of Atholl between 1738 and 1830.

There are plenty of good circular signposted walks in the woods around here and along the river bank, with carpets of bluebells in late spring, and red squirrels to look out for – a leaflet from the tourist office gives full details. One walk leads through mixed woodland along the River Braan and up to the folly of the Hermitage, or Ossian's Hall, set above the Black Linn Falls.

Little Dunkeld is the last resting place of the great Scottish fiddler, Neil Gow (1727–1807), who composed many dance tunes and fine airs and was famous throughout Britain for his skill. His violin is on display at Blair Castle.

KILLIN MAP REF NN5733

The village of Killin is set beneath the hills where the River Dochart tumbles over an extensive waterfall and into the western end of Loch Tay. Once home to the MacNabs, it is at the heart of the ancient district of Breadalbane, and has now become a popular walking, fishing and touring centre. The 79-mile (127km) Rob Roy Way long-distance path between Drymen and Pitochry passes through the town. The Breadalbane Folklore Centre located in St Fillan's Mill shares its premises with the local tourist office, and offers an intriguing insight into Scottish legends of kelpies, brownies and other mythical creatures. The mill originally powered machines for the weaving of tweed. The ruins of 16th-century Finlarig Castle, a Campbell stronghold, stand at the head of the loch. It has what are said to be the only surviving remains in the country of a beheading pit, reserved especially for the execution of the gentry.

The National Trust for Scotland is noted for its preservation of some grand castles, but lists some more modest dwellings, too. One of the humblest is along the narrow Glen Lochay Road, just north of Killin. Moirlanich Longhouse is a long, low 19th-century farmhouse, built with a cruck frame. At least three generations of the Robertson family lived here, until the 1960s, and the house has been preserved, complete with a 'hingin' lum' (suspended chimney) and traditional wooden box beds.

The view from Killin up Loch Tay is dominated by Ben Lawers, at 3,984 feet (1,214m) the highest peak in the area. It is known for its delicate alpine flora, and with the neighbouring Tarmachan range, is a popular focus for walkers. The area is a national nature reserve.

DOCHART FALLS, KILLIN

Queen Elizabeth Forest Park

The Loch Ard Forest in the hilly Trossachs region of Central Scotland is part of the Queen Elizabeth Forest Park. The route soon leaves the tourist-friendly village of Aberfoyle and rambles through thick forests and around the hills that pepper this area, known affectionately by many Scots as the 'foothills of the Highlands'. Look out for grazing red and roe deer, capercaillie, wood ants and stunning barn owls.

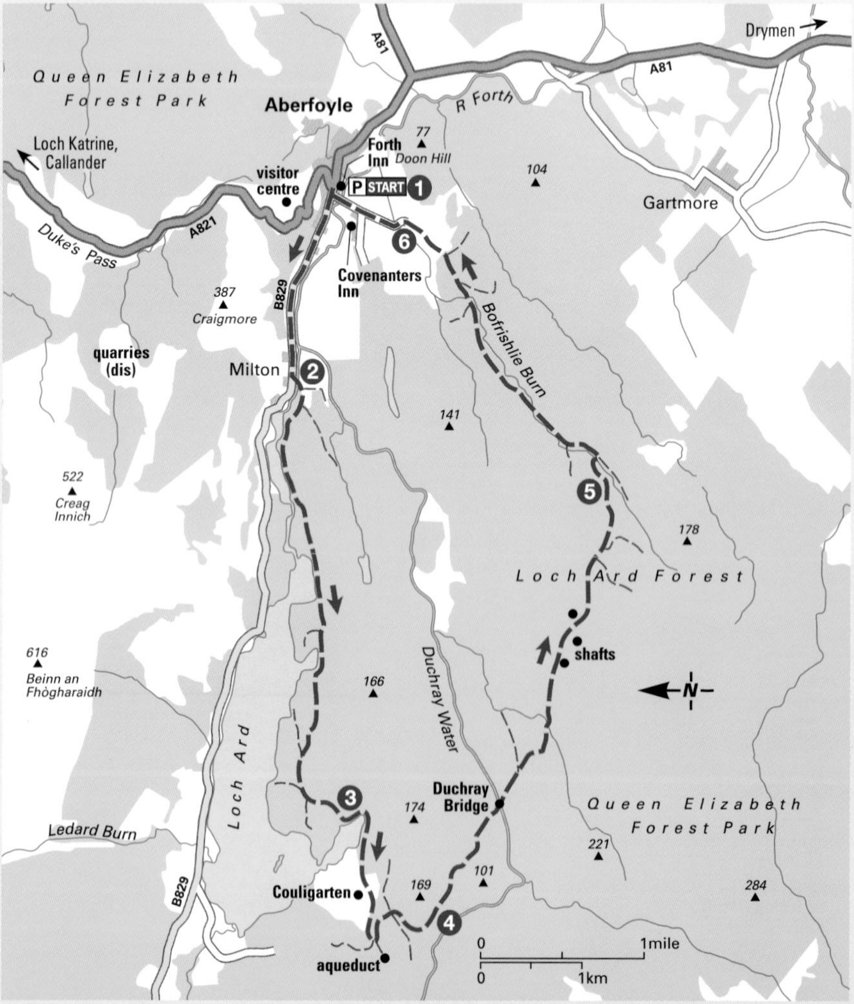

Route Directions

1 From the family-run Forth Inn head towards Aberfoyle's main car park behind the inn and then turn right past the cars towards a small exit. Take a right turn and head up the minor road to a junction where you turn left on to an even quieter road that meanders west in search of Loch Ard.

2 Before going into the hamlet of Milton leave the road to take the track to the left, which curls around towards the loch. You are now in the forest proper so take care on the looser woodland tracks as you head west, snatching tempting glimpses of the loch as you go.

3 After a short section deep inside the forest, the track drops back down to the loch at Couligarten. Look out for a left turn just past Couligarten – if you get to the aqueduct you have come too far.

4 The path rises through the forest cutting and between a series of low wooded hills that lie to the left of Duchray Water. You cross over the waterway at the Duchray Bridge after a zig-zag section. Continue on the trail as it starts to curve back towards Aberfoyle village.

5 After tracking a section that traverses some old mine shafts you then pick up the Bofrishlie Burn (burn is Scots for stream), which tumbles down towards Aberfoyle; avoid the tracks that break off the main route as they lead deeper into the forest and you risk getting lost.

6 As the route leaves the forest behind it becomes surfaced and passes to the west of Doon Hill (the 'hill of the fairies') just before The Covenanters Inn hotel comes into view on the left. The Forth Inn is only a short cycle away now across the River Forth, accessible via the right turn into the main village car park from where you set out.

Route facts

DISTANCE/TIME 11 miles (17.5km) 2h

MAP OS Explorer 365 The Trossachs

START The Forth Inn (ask permission to park), grid ref: NN523010

TRACKS Road, forest tracks (good condition), some quite steep rises

GETTING TO THE START The Forth Inn is just off the A81 main road through Aberfoyle, on the left as you come from the M9 motorway, by the village's main car park.

CYCLE HIRE Trossachs Holiday Park, Aberfoyle. Tel 01877 382614

THE PUB The Forth Inn, Main Street, Aberfoyle. Tel: 01877 382372

Visit

STORIES IN STONE
Stones and cross-slabs carved in Pictish times are a feature of the landscape over to the west and south of Kirriemuir. Some of the best have been gathered together in the former schoolhouse at Meigle, where they form a fascinating collection dating from the 8th to the 10th centuries. Along with favourite subjects such as salmon, dogs and horsemen, there are stranger creatures to discover, such as birds with bulbous eyes.

KIRRIEMUIR MAP REF NO3854

Kirriemuir is the gateway to the great Glens of Angus, the long valleys which stretch north into the open moorland of the Grampian Mountains, forming the southern edge of the mighty Cairngorms National Park. The range includes Glen Esk, Glen Clova and Glen Prosen, and they all offer superb hill-walking, with Glen Clova giving access to remote Glen Doll. The glens are all home to red and black grouse, golden eagles, ptarmigans and capercaillies, red and roe deer. Antarctic explorer Robert Falcon Scott and Edward Wilson, the expedition's doctor and artist, came to the area to plan their ill-fated voyage to the South Pole, and are commemorated by a memorial cairn in Glen Prosen.

Kirriemuir itself is an industrious red sandstone town, built on the revenues of weaving and farming. The town hosts an annual walking festival in May and June, but its main claim to fame is its associations with the playwright and novelist J M Barrie. The creator of Peter Pan was born here in 1860, the son of a weaver and one of ten children, and his birthplace is now an evocative museum. The wash-house round the back of the property served as Barrie's first theatre, and may have inspired the Wendy House in *Peter Pan* (1904). Although he lived for most of his life in London, Barrie wrote with great affection about the small-town life of Kirriemuir, disguised as 'Thrums' in his tales. In 1930 Barrie presented the community with a novel gift after they had honoured him with the freedom of the town: a camera obscura on nearby Kirrie Hill, for far-reaching views over the surrounding countryside (check at the birthplace for opening times).

About 5 miles (8km) to the south of Kirriemuir lies Glamis Castle, family seat of the Earls of Strathmore and Kinghorne, and the childhood home of the late Queen Elizabeth, the Queen Mother. With its multiple turrets and fairytale battlements Glamis Castle (pronounced 'Glahms') is a vision of what a Scottish castle should look like, and the interior is equally fabulous too, with moulded plaster ceilings and fine panelling. At its core is a medieval tower house, dating back to around 1372. The surrounding parkland is well worth exploring, with its formal Italian garden and a pinetum. For a total contrast, six 18th-century cottages in the nearby village house the Angus Folk Museum, showing how the rural community lived.

PERTH MAP REF NO1223

The Roman settlement of Perth was founded on the banks of the River Tay in the 1st century; in the Middle Ages it became the capital of Scotland. Today it is a lively city at the centre of a thriving and established farming community, its compact core offering great shopping and bohemian cafés that spill out onto the pavements. Open-top bus tours from the railway station are a good way to gain an overview. With its theatre, City Hall, a brand new concert hall and other venues, not to mention galleries and cinemas, Perth is an active centre for music and the arts, culminating in a lively festival in May.

Perth's extensive parks are headed by the North Inch and the South Inch, beside the river, and there are several gardens to explore in the area, including Branklyn, which is specially noted for its blue Himalayan poppies (*Meconopsis*).

In recent years Perth has developed as the adventure capital of Scotland, with an ever-longer list of adventure sports and activities to take you out and about across the region. So if the more traditional sports of fishing, golf, pony trekking, mountain biking and hill-hiking seem tame, you can get your adrenalin rush by quad biking, off-road driving, abseiling, canoeing, waterskiing, cliff-jumping, white-water rafting or even paintballing – and that's just for a start. The tourist office has more details.

Scone Palace is on the outskirts of the city, a privately owned mansion rich in history. It remains the family seat of the Earls of Mansfield, and the ancient crowning place of Scottish kings since Robert the Bruce. Forty two kings were crowned on the Stone of Scone – unfortunately the original block is held for safekeeping in Edinburgh Castle (since its theft in the 1950s), so what you see here is a replica. There are fine bed hangings in the house, which were embroidered by Mary, Queen of Scots herself. The gardens and grounds are attractively planted, and a modern addition is the beech maze, planted in a suitably Scottish tartan pattern.

PITLOCHRY MAP REF NN9457

This bustling town in the wooded valley of the River Tummel is based around one long main street, running parallel with the river, and lined with shops and eating places. The geographical heart of Scotland, it first appeared on the map when General Wade built a military road through here, and it has been a popular holiday resort since the 19th century.

A footbridge leads across the river to the Festival Theatre, with its Explorers' Garden, opened in 2003 to celebrate 300 years of botanical exploration and collection of artefacts from around the world by Scots. The theatre is a popular venue for an ever-changing programme of drama and concerts. There is a view from the footbridge to the salmon ladder, which was installed as part of a hydroelectric dam system along the river and which also created Loch Faskally, a local beauty spot. Learn more at the Scottish Hydroelectric Visitor Centre, which gives access to an observation window where you can watch the wild salmon jumping (usually between April and October). Pitlochry boasts two distilleries, which both welcome visitors: the Blair Athol Distillery in the town centre, and tiny Edradour on the outskirts.

Just to the north of the town is the conservation village of Moulin, with its 17th-century church and ruined castle in the shadow of Ben Vrackie. The writer Robert Louis Stevenson stayed here in 1881, and described it as a 'sweet spot'.

Some 3miles (4.8km) north of Pitlochry is the narrow, wooded gorge of Killiecrankie, on the River Garry. This was the site of a battle in 1689 when a Jacobite army defeated government troops. There is a scenic walk of about a mile (1.6km) here.

Continue north and you'll reach Blair Castle, a white-painted mansion in a majestic setting of trees and gardens, with hills behind. It's been the ancestral home of the Dukes and Earls of Atholl for more than 700 years, and can claim its own private army. The castle itself is located on the main route north through the Highlands which made it a strategic prize in several major conflicts. Bonnie Prince Charlie slept in the little, now tartan-clad tower room in 1745. The exterior of the castle reflects a Victorian make-over in 1863. Inside are wonderful artefacts, plasterwork and paintings.

THE TROSSACHS

The Trossachs is an area of outstanding natural beauty in central Scotland, now with protected status as the main sector of the Loch Lomond and the Trossachs National Park. Scotland's first such designated park, its land stretches for 720 square miles (1,865sq km) from the Argyll Forest Park in the west over to Callander in the east, and from Killin and Tyndrum in the north to Balloch in the south, at the foot of Loch Lomond. The Trossachs is the region lying to the east of Loch Lomond which was first 'discovered' by travellers in the late 18th century, and was popularised for a wider audience as a thrilling backdrop to the novels of Sir Walter Scott (1771–1832). Scott's famous poem, 'The Lady of the Lake' (1810), was set in identifiable and accessible places across the Trossachs, and brought tourists to the area.

The village of Aberfoyle is the key to this region, giving easy access to the wooded hills of the Queen Elizabeth Forest Park and the peak of Ben Venue (2,391 feet/729m), and Loch Katrine to the north. There are great opportunities for walking and cycling, including a pretty cycle route that runs through the Forest Park and continues along the shores of Loch Venachar and Loch Lubnaig to Balquhidder, Lochearnhead and Killin. The Trossachs Discovery visitor centre in Aberfoyle is a mine of information about activities in the area. The Scottish Wool Centre behind it offers an entertaining Sheepdog Show, as well as a chance to see lambs and sheep shearing in season.

Loch Katrine, at the heart of the Trossachs, is a loch of clear, sparkling water studded by pretty islands and surrounded by woodland and mountains, and looks almost too good to be true. In fact, it serves central Glasgow with fresh water, and part of its peaceful aspect comes from the fact that only one motorised boat is permitted upon its waters: the elegant old steamship, SS *Sir Walter Scott*. You can hire a bicycle at the pier and follow the route round the northern shore of the loch.

Trossachs Trail

Starting from attractive Killin village, with the Falls of Dochart on its doorstep, this drive explores the varied and magnificent scenery of Scotland's first designated national park of Loch Lomond and the Trossachs.

Route Directions

1 Leave the hill-walking centre of Killin on the A827, and follow this northeast for 17 miles (27km) to Kenmore.
As you pass Loch Tay on the right, the big, bare-looking mountain of Ben Lawers (3,984 feet/1,214m) looms up to your left. The area is now a National Nature Reserve and is celebrated for its Arctic and alpine flora, which thrives on the lime-rich soils. Look for mountain hares on the high ground. Kenmore supports a popular watersports centre and on the loch is the Scottish Crannog Centre.

2 Continue on the A827 for 6 miles (10km) to Aberfeldy .
Pass a memorial of 1887 to the men of the Black Watch on the southern side of the bridge. The Black Watch regiment was enrolled into the British Army in 1739, and took its name from the soldiers' dark tartan, which was carefully selected to differentiate them from the Guardsmen, or 'Red Soldiers'.

3 Leave by the A826, and follow this wild road up over the high moors. Turn right at the A822, then right at the A85 and follow this into Crieff. Continue on the A85 for 19 miles (31km) through Comrie to Lochearnhead.
This small town at the western tip of Lochearn grew when the railway was built through Glen Ogle, which lies to the north and links up with Killin, passing to a height of 948 feet (289m). Edinample Castle (private), a castellated mansion of 1630, lies where the Burn of Ample runs into the loch.

4 Leave by the A84 and follow it for 14 miles (23km) southward to Callander, passing a turning right to Balquhidder, where outlaw Rob Roy MacGregor (1671–1734) is buried in the churchyard. Continue along the A84 and then turn left at the A821. After passing the turreted mansion of Tigh Mor, follow signs (right) to Loch Katrine.
Leave your car in the parking area at the end and take a walk or bicycle ride beside this loch, 9 miles (15km) long, whose island-studded beauty became legendary after Sir Walter Scott's description in 'The Lady of the Lake'. While recreation is to the fore as visitors come in droves to enjoy the scene and take a ride on the steamer, the loch also has a serious practical function, supplying central Glasgow with fresh water via an underground pipeway some 35 miles (56km) long.

5 Return to the A821 and turn right. Follow the A821 for 7 miles (11km) over the hills on the Duke's Pass, and continue through the dense Achray Forest to the little town of Aberfoyle.
Aberfoyle is surrounded by the pine trees of the Queen Elizabeth Forest Park, and the visitor centre, situated a mile to the north has comprehensive information about the area's walking and cycling routes. The Scottish Wool Centre in Aberfoyle attracts many visitors.

6 Continue on the A821 and the A81. At the intersection with the A811, turn right to pass Drymen, and then go through Gartocharn.

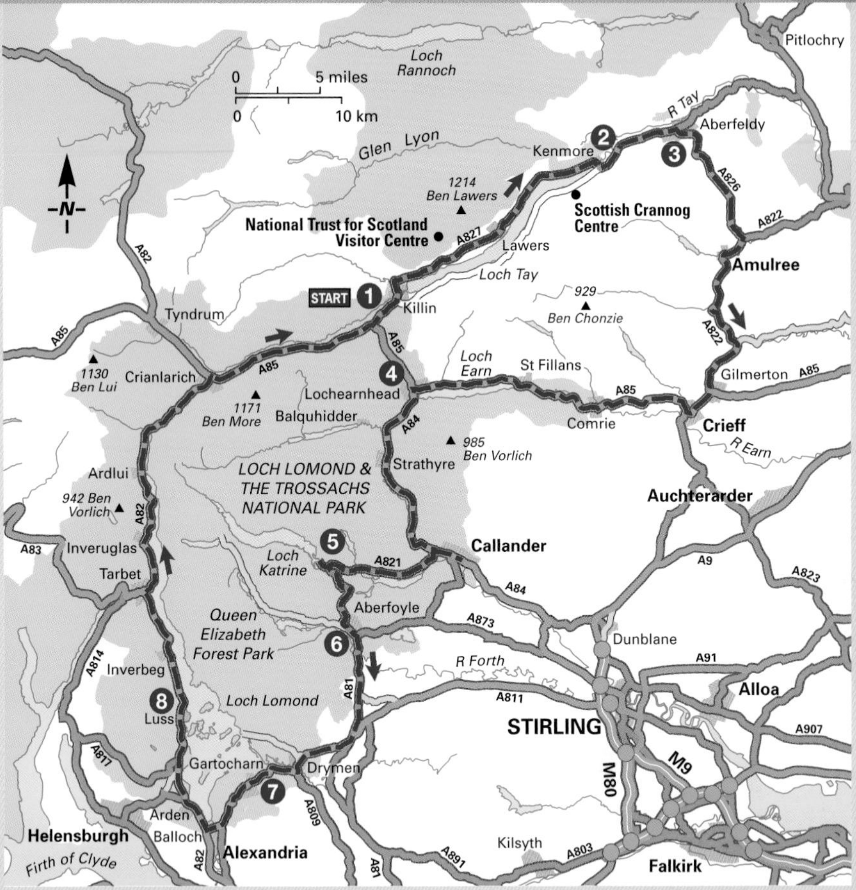

Quiet little Gartocharn is best known for the wonderful view up Loch Lomond from the hill, Duncryne (462feet/142m), known fondly to locals as the 'Dumpling', behind the village.

7 Continue on the A811 through Balloch and turn right at the A82. Follow this main route north, and after about 9 miles (14.5km) pass the turning to the pretty village of Luss. Continue on by the west shore of the Loch as it narrows.

Lying near the foot of Loch Lomond, Balloch has an ultra-modern shopping mall with fantastic views of the loch. Pass Inverbeg where you can catch a ferry across the loch to the isolated settlement of Rowardennan.

8 Rejoin the A82 and keep travelling up the west shore of the loch. After Ardlui, the mountains become more rugged as you continue up Glen Falloch to Crianlarich. Turn right here on to the A85. Go through Glen Dochart. Pass Loch Lubhair on the left, with Ben More (3,842 feet/ 1,171m) on the right. Turn left at the A827 to return to Killin.

PLACES OF INTEREST

Angus Folk Museum (NTS)
Kirkwynd, Glamis.
Tel: 0844 493 2141

J M Barrie's Birthplace (NTS)
9 Brechin Road, Kirriemuir.
Tel: 0844 493 2142

Blair Athol Distillery
Perth Road, Pitlochry.
Tel: 01796 482003

Ben Lawers National Nature Reserve (NTS)
Off A827, 6 miles (9.7km) northeast of Killin.
Tel: 0844 493 2136

The Black Watch Regimental Museum
Balhousie Castle, North Inch, Perth. Tel: 01738 638152; www.theblackwatch.co.uk

Blair Castle
Blair Atholl, just off A9.
Tel: 01796 481207; www.blair-castle.co.uk

Branklyn Garden (NTS)
116 Dundee Road, Perth.
Tel: 01738 625535

Castle Menzies
Weem, by Aberfeldy.
Tel: 01887 820982

Dewar's World of Whisky
Aberfeldy Distillery, Aberfeldy.
Tel: 01887 822010; www.dewarswow.com

RRS *Discovery*
Dundee.
Tel: 01382 309060; www.rrsdiscovery.com

Doune Castle (HS)
Castle Road, Doune.
Tel: 01786 841742

Drummond Castle Gardens
Muthill, Crieff.
Tel: 01764 681433; www.drummoncastlegardens.co.uk

Earthquake House
Comrie.

Edradour Distillery
Pitlochry. Tel: 01796 472095; www.edradour.co.uk

Famous Grouse Experience
The Hosh, Crieff.
Tel: 01764 656565; www.thefamousgrouse.com

Frigate *Unicorn*
Discovery Point, Dundee.
Tel: 01382 200900; www.frigateunicorn.org

Glamis Castle
Glamis. Tel: 01307 840393; www.glamis-castle.co.uk

The Hermitage (NTS)
by Dunkeld. Tel: 0844 493 2192

Inchmahome Priory (HS)
Lake of Menteith.
Tel: 01877 385294

Innerpeffray Library
5 miles (8km)from Crieff, off B8062. Tel: 01764 652819

Killiecrankie Visitor Centre (NTS)
3 miles (5km) north of Pitlochry. Tel: 0844 493 2194

Loch of the Lowes Visitor Centre
Off A923 northeast of Dunkeld. Tel: 01350 727337; www.swt.org.uk

Meigle Sculptured Stone Museum (HS)
Blairgowrie.
Tel: 01828 640612

Moirlanich Longhouse (NTS)
Near to Killin.
Tel: 0844 493 2136

Perth Museum & Art Gallery
78 George Street, Perth.
Tel: 01738 632488; www.pkc.gov.uk

Queen's View Visitor Centre
Allean, 7 miles (11.3km) west of Pitlochry on B8019.
Tel: 01350 727284; www.forestry.gov.uk

Scone Palace
Scone, by Perth.
Tel: 01738 552300; www.scone-palace.net

Scottish Crannog Centre
South Loch Tay, Kenmore.
Tel: 01887 830583; www.crannog.co.uk

Scottish Hydroelectric Visitor Centre
Pitlochry. Tel: 01796 473152; www.scottish-southern.co.uk

Scottish Wool Centre
Aberfoyle. Tel: 01877 382850

Verdant Works
West Henderson's Wynd, Dundee. Tel: 01382 309060; www.rrsdiscovery.com

FOR CHILDREN

Beatrix Potter Exhibition & Garden
Birnham Arts and Conference Centre, Station Road, Birnham, by Dunkeld.
Tel: 01350 727674; www.birnhaminstitute.com

Camperdown Wildlife Centre
Camperdown Country Park,

Dundee. Tel: 01382 431811; www.dundeecity.gov.uk/camperdown

Drummond Trout Farm & Fishery
Comrie, off A85.
Tel: 01567 830400; www.drummondtroutfarm.co.uk

Sensation
Greenmarket, Dundee.
Tel: 01382 228800; www.sensation.org.uk

SHOPPING

House of Bruar
by Blair Atholl.
Tel: 0845 1360111; www.houseofbruar.com

Mains of Taymouth Delicatessen and Retail
Kenmore
Tel: 01887 830756; www.taymouthcourtyard.com

Perth Farmers' Market
First Sat each month; www.perthfarmersmarket.co.uk

SPORTS & ACTIVITIES

ADVENTURE SPORTS

Croft-na-Caber
Kenmore, Loch Tay.
Tel: 01887 830588; www.breadalbane.com

Highland Safaris
Drumdewan, Aberfeldy.
Tel: 01887 820071; www.highlandsafaris.net

Loch Tay Boating Centre
Pier Road, Kenmore.
Tel: 01887 830291; www.loch-tay.co.uk

BOAT TRIPS

SS *Sir Walter Scott*
Trossachs Pier Complex.
Tel: 01877 332000; www.lochkatrine.com

CYCLING

Escape Route
3 Atholl Road, Pitlochry.
Tel: 01796 473859; www.escape-route.biz

Katrinewheelz
Trossachs Pier Complex, Loch Katrine.
Tel: 01877 376366; www.lochkatrine.co.uk

FISHING

Lake of Menteith Fisheries
Ryeyards, Port of Menteith.
Tel: 01877 385664; www.menteith-fisheries.co.uk

GOLF

Crieff Golf Course
Ferntower, Perth Road.
Tel: 01764 652909; www.crieffgolf.co.uk

Gleneagles Hotel and Resort
Auchterarder.
Tel: 0800 389 38737; www.gleneagles.com

Pitlochry Golf Course
Golf Course Road, Pitlochry.
Tel: 01796 472792; www.pitlochrygolf.co.uk

HORSE-RIDING

Millhorn Riding Centre
Bendochy, Coupar Angus.
Tel: 01828 626172; www.millhornridingcentre.co.uk

WALKING

Cateran Trail
Circular trail from Blairgowrie, 64 miles (103km).
www.pkct.org/caterantrail

Loch Lomond and the Trossachs National Park
www.lochlomond-trossachs.org

Rob Roy Way
Drymen to Pitlochry.
92 miles (148km).
www.robroyway.com

CUSTOMS & EVENTS

Blair Castle
Glenfiddich Piping Championships, end Oct
Atholl Gathering and Highland Games, end May

Comrie
Flambeaux Procession, 31 Dec

Crieff
Highland Gathering, Aug

Kirriemuir
Angus Glens Walking Festival, end May, Jun

Perth
Festival of the Arts, May
Highland Games, Aug

Pitlochry
Highland Games, Sep

Tea Rooms

The Gleneagles Hotel

**Auchterarder,
Perth & Kinross PH3 1NF
Tel: 01764 662231;
www.gleneagles.com**

With an international reputation for high standards and its championship golf course, this grand hotel is one of the finest in Scotland. It's main restaurant has a coveted four AA rosettes, but if dining here seems a little over the top, why not treat yourself to afternoon tea. If the standard package with delicious cakes, sandwiches, pastries and scones isn't enough, try the champagne version with smoked salmon and canapés served before the sweet delights.

House of Bruar

**by Blair Atholl, Perthshire
PH18 5TW
Tel: 0845 136 0111;
www.houseofbruar.com**

This upmarket shopping outlet boasts an excellent self-service restaurant, where you can collapse with your purchases and enjoy a decent tea or coffee, along with freshly baked scones, biscuits and cakes. If you're making a day of it, they serve excellent hot meals as well as home-made soup, gourmet sandwiches and seafood salads. Stock up on supplies to take home from the Food Hall next door.

The Watermill

**Mill Street, Aberfeldy
PH15 2BG
Tel: 01887 822896; www.aberfeldywatermill.com**

This extensive converted watermill complex includes a bookshop, music shop and art gallery, all infused with the aroma of fresh coffee. Enjoy a fruit smoothie on the terrace, or a speciality coffee with your cake – all the products are locally sourced or organic where possible. The old waterwheel is still used to power the lighting!

Pubs

Cross Keys Hotel

**Main Street, Kippen FK8 3DN
Tel: 01786 870293**

The small village of Kippen is some 10 miles (16km) west of Stirling and just off the A811. Close by, Burnside Wood is perfect for walking and nature trails. This friendly gastropub on the high street, dating from 1703, offers excellent home-made food, including home-smoked duck breast and chilli crab linguini. Beers include Harviestoun Bitter & Twisted. Children are welcome, and dogs are allowed too.

Killiecrankie House Hotel

**Killiecrankie PH16 5LG
Tel: 01796 473220;
www.killiecrankiehotel.co.uk**

This sprawling country house hotel at the northern end of the Killiecrankie Pass offers great informal dining in its cosy, mahogany-panelled Covenanters' Bar (as well as a top-notch restaurant). Try the honey-roast ham salad, or perhaps the game pie. The produce is local, and fruit and vegetables are often fresh from the hotel's garden. Dogs are welcome.

Moulin Hotel

**11–13 Kirkmichael Road,
Moulin PH16 5EH
Tel: 01796 472196;
www.moulinhotel.co.uk**

Just outside Pitlochry on the A924 stands this imposing old village inn, offering Highland hospitality, home-brewed beer and good food. It's at the foot of Ben Vrackie, so good walking country is on the doorstep. Food is served all day, with blazing log fires in the winter and a lovely courtyard garden for summer. The menu might include seafood pancakes and haggis and game casserole. From the pub's micro-brewery you can try local favourites such as Old Remedial.

KINNOULL HILL, PERTH

LOCH CRERAN, OBAN

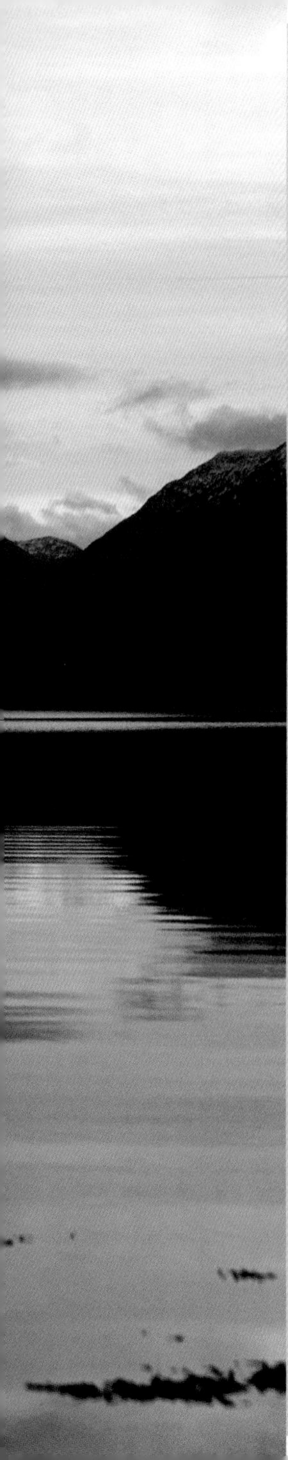

Argyll, Mull & Western Highlands

The indentations of western Scotland's rugged coastline characterise this diverse region, with the grandeur and majesty of Glen Coe and the craggy mountains and valleys of the north contrasting with the more open, hilly landscapes of the south. Great sea lochs spread their narrowing fingers inland, creating isolated and island-bound communities, and havens for wildlife. There is ancient history to discover at Kilmartin and Iona, and industrial history in Scotland's vibrant second city, Glasgow.

KILCHURN CASTLE, LOCH AWE

DUNOON PIER

GLASGOW

GLEN COE

Unmissable attractions

Cruise across the still waters of Loch Lomond and visit popular Balloch Country Park at its southern end...witness the scene of the bloody massacre of the Macdonald clan at Glen Coe...admire the rhododendron blooms in the gardens of Brodick Castle at the foot of Goatfell Mountain...attend the Cowal Highland Gathering at Dunoon where pipers come from all parts of the world to compete against each other...spend some time in cultural and cosmopolitan Glasgow and visit the ultra-modern Science Centre and the Glasgow Tower...step into the ancient jail at Inveraray and discover the life of a prisoner...take a ferry ride to Iona from the little harbour at Tobermory, on the Isle of Mull, to visit the ancient burial ground of King Macbeth.

1

2

3

1 **Luma Light Factory, Glasgow**
The distinctive 1930s art deco former light bulb factory has been converted into flats, but it retains the stylish glass tower as a staircase. Now known as the Luma Tower, the conversion has won several architectural awards.

2 **Glen Coe**
A lone piper plays a lament in the pass of Glen Coe. It was at this spot in 1692 that 38 members of the Macdonald clan were murdered by their guests, on the orders of the government. The area has long been popular with walkers and climbers and now attracts skiers, too.

3 **Crinan Canal**
The village of Cairnbaan sits at the edge of the Crinan Canal. Above the village are a series of probably Iron Age cup and ring marks in the rock.

4 **Loch Lomond**
A view to Loch Lomond across the plain below Duncryne Hill, which is also known to locals as 'The Dumpling'.

5 **Isle of Mull**
Campers on the shore of Loch Na Keal on Mull off Scotland's west coast. The sea loch here is popular for birding. Minke whales, dolphins and porpoises visit in the summer.

6 **Kilchurn Castle, Loch Awe**
One of the most romantically situated castles in Scotland, the ruins of Kilchurn stand out on a peninsula on Loch Awe. What's left of the 15th-century castle can be reached by ferry or on foot.

ARDNAMURCHAN & MORVERN

MAP REF NM5567/NM6745

You can go no further west on mainland Britain than Ardnamurchan Point, with its spectacular views over to Mull, Coll and Tiree. The whole peninsula, with its rocky hills and desolate moorland, gale-blown trees and pretty heather-capped promontories, has an 'end-of-the-world' feeling. The main road mostly hugs the northern shore of Loch Sunart, rich in birdlife, and you can take a minor road to Ardnamurchan's north coast as the main road passes round Beinn nan Losgann, or continue to the little crofting village of Kilchoan, where a ferry goes to Tobermory on Mull. The 13th-century Mingary Castle, built on its sheer rock to guard the entrance to Loch Sunart, is the place where King James IV finally accepted the submission of the Lord of the Isles in 1495; Hanoverian troops built barracks inside it 350 years later.

Make a detour to Sanna Bay for views to Muck, Rum and Canna and for superb wild flowers by the beach. A lighthouse stands guard on the furthest tip of the peninsula, with access inside in summer – it's a good place for spotting seals and otters, if you're lucky.

Morvern, across Loch Sunart, is a rugged land with gentler green glens. Lochaline, a popular yachting haven, is reached either by road along Glen Gleann, or by ferry from the Isle of Mull. Visit the remains of Ardtornish Castle, east of the village. The silica sands at Lochaline have been quarried commercially for manufacturing optical glass. Fiunary, along the Sound of Mull, was the birthplace of George Macleod, founder of the Iona Community. It is also the source of a haunting lament, the song 'Farewell to Fiunary'. Caisteal nan Con is a small fortress guarding the Sound of Mull. The road ends some 4 miles (6.4km) beyond, near Drimnin, with views towards Tobermory.

ARRAN, ISLE OF

MAP REF NR9536

Generations of Clydesiders have enjoyed holidays on this attractive island, caught between the Ayrshire coast and the Kintyre Peninsula, yet it remains largely unspoiled. The Highland Boundary Fault runs through the island, and while the mountain of Goat Fell (2,867 feet/874m) dominates the skyline to the north, the south is much more level. This reflects the geology of the country as a whole, and Arran is often tagged 'Scotland in Miniature'. Glen Rosa offers fairly easy walking, while Goat Fell and Glen Sannox are more rugged, and there are plenty of opportunities for a range of other outdoor activities, including golf and pony trekking, around the island. Brodick is the biggest town, with villages catering for visitors scattered round the 56-mile (90km) coastline.

The red sandstone Brodick Castle is the island's biggest single attraction, with its extensive collection of porcelain and silver, some 19th-century sporting pictures and trophies, and beautiful country park of meadows and woodland. The gardens include a world-renowned collection of rhododendrons. The seat of the Dukes of Hamilton, the estate has a history that dates back 800 years.

The legacy of much earlier settlers may be seen in the chambered cairns at Clachaig, Whiting Bay and other sites, and also in the stone circles on Machrie Moor. The standing stones date from the Bronze Age but there is also evidence that the site was previously occupied in the neolithic era.

In recent years the island has developed a name for its food produce, which includes cheese and smoked meats. Around the courtyard of Home Farm, just north of Brodick, you can see the cheese being made at the Island Cheese Company, and you can purchase delicately smoked fish, rich game and free-range poultry next door at Creelers Smokehouse (or sample it in Creeler's Seafood Restaurant). The fragrant soaps of Arran Aromatics share the same site. Arran Fine Foods, at Lamlash, sells a range of locally produced mustards and preserves. The island's distillery, based at Lochranza, only opened in the 1990s.

Ferries to Arran operate from Ardrossan (year-round) and Claonaig, by Skipness (summer). The Ayrshire coast between here and Prestwick Airport is famous worldwide for the quality of its golf courses, centring on Troon.

Insight

BRUCE AND THE SPIDER

In 1307, on his way back from exile on Rathlin Island, off Northern Ireland, Robert the Bruce mustered his troops in Glen Cloy, on Arran, before heading to the Scottish mainland to try once more to oust the English and claim the throne. According to legend, he was roused from despair and inspired to fight once more – and succeed this time – by watching a spider, spinning its web and succeeding only on the seventh attempt to attach its thread. In another version of the story, he watched the spider in a cave near to Blackwaterfoot on Arran, known to this day as the King's Caves.

Insight

LANGUAGE OF THE LAND

In Scotland lakes are lochs, and 'ben' means mountain. Like many Highland place-names, these are Gaelic words, and often give an idea of the kind of place they refer to – 'kin' (Gaelic ceann), for example, means head, so Kinloch means the top of a lake, while 'inver' (inbhir) denotes an outlet – Inverness is where the River Ness meets the sea. 'Tarbert' (or 'Tarbet') means isthmus or crossing place. Other pointers include 'ard', a height, 'ban' meaning white; 'beg', confusingly meaning little, and 'more', meaning great. It all adds another dimension to the landscape.

CRINAN CANAL MAP REF NR8292

In 1847 Queen Victoria and Prince Albert sailed the 9 miles (14.5km) of the Crinan Canal aboard the barge *Sunbeam* – a journey followed later in the century by MacBrayne's steamers in order to sell 'Royal Route' excursions from Glasgow to Oban. Today you are most likely to see pleasure craft negotiating the canal's 15 locks, but its original purpose was to enable merchant traffic to and from the Western Isles to avoid the hazardous voyage around the Mull of Kintyre. Two famous engineers worked on the Crinan Canal, which opened in 1801. John Rennie was responsible for the original engineering work, and Thomas Telford solved problems with the water supply.

From the basin at Ardrishaig, where it leaves Loch Fyne, the canal hugs the wooded hillsides as it climbs up to its highest point of 64 feet (19.5m). On the hills above Cairnbaan are reservoirs that constantly replenish the water down in the canal as it descends underneath the unusual hand-wound rolling bridge at Dunardry. Beyond this the landscape then opens out into the flat marshland near to the River Add estuary. The canal ends at the picturesque haven of Crinan Harbour, with beautiful views over the Sound of Jura. Enjoy a drink and snack here at the Crinan Hotel. With some luck you may find a 'puffer' in the harbour to remind you of the canal's past glories.

DUNOON MAP REF NS1776

Paddle steamers used to bring huge crowds from Gourock to Dunoon, and there are still regular ferry services here. On the grassy headland between the town's two bays are the remains of the 13th-century royal castle, largely destroyed in 1685. Below is the 1896 statue of Burns's love, Highland Mary, erected to mark the centenary of the poet's death. Dunoon is busiest each year during late August for the Cowal Highland Gathering, when more than 150 pipe bands from all over the world compete for prestigious trophies.

Morag's Fairy Glen, off the road south from Dunoon, has shaded walks along the Berry Burn, but for more expansive views, continue onward to Toward Point lighthouse (not open) at the southern end of the A815, where you can look out across the water to Bute and down to Largs. In the grounds of the stout 19th-century Castle Toward, now an education centre, is a ruined 15th-century tower house, somewhat confusingly called Toward Castle. One of the most vile atrocities of the Civil War began here, when Campbell of Ardkinglas besieged the Lamonts, who were Stuart loyalists. Although guaranteed safety, 36 Lamont men were taken to Dunoon and hanged – a monument in Tom-a-Mhoid Road marks the place.

This area is rich in ancient sites. Near Sandbank, on the shore of Holy Loch, are the huge stones forming Adam's Grave, a remaining neolithic burial chamber, and you can take a trail from near Ardnadam Farm to see the ancient field boundaries and the site of a prehistoric enclosure.

Bute has been the holiday playground for generations of Glaswegians, most of whom arrive at Rothesay on the ferry from Wemyss Bay. Standing on the Firth of Clyde, Rothesay has a late 19th-century atmosphere created by its solid, mostly Victorian houses and decorative Winter Gardens (now housing a visitor centre), but much more ancient are the impressive ruins of the moated and circular 13th-century Rothesay Castle, where some restoration took place in the 19th and 20th centuries.

The island largely consists of green and fertile hills, with superb views across the narrow Kyles of Bute to the mainland and to mountainous Arran. Just off the east coast road is one of Bute's hidden gems, the extraordinary Victorian Gothic Mount Stuart House, surrounded by extensive gardens that lead down to the shore.

147
contention

Along the Crinan Canal and Around Mòine Mhór

A lengthy but easy stroll along the 19th-century Crinan Canal, which allows easy passage from Loch Fyne to the Sound of Jura, avoiding the lengthy voyage around the Mull of Kintyre. The walk also passes through Mòine Mhór (managed by Scottish Natural Heritage), Scotland's last wild peat bog, a birders' paradise, echoing with the distinctive cry of the curlew as it returns each spring. At Bellanoch look to see how the engineers cut the canal into the hillside when it proved impossible to lay a foundation on the Mòine Mhór.

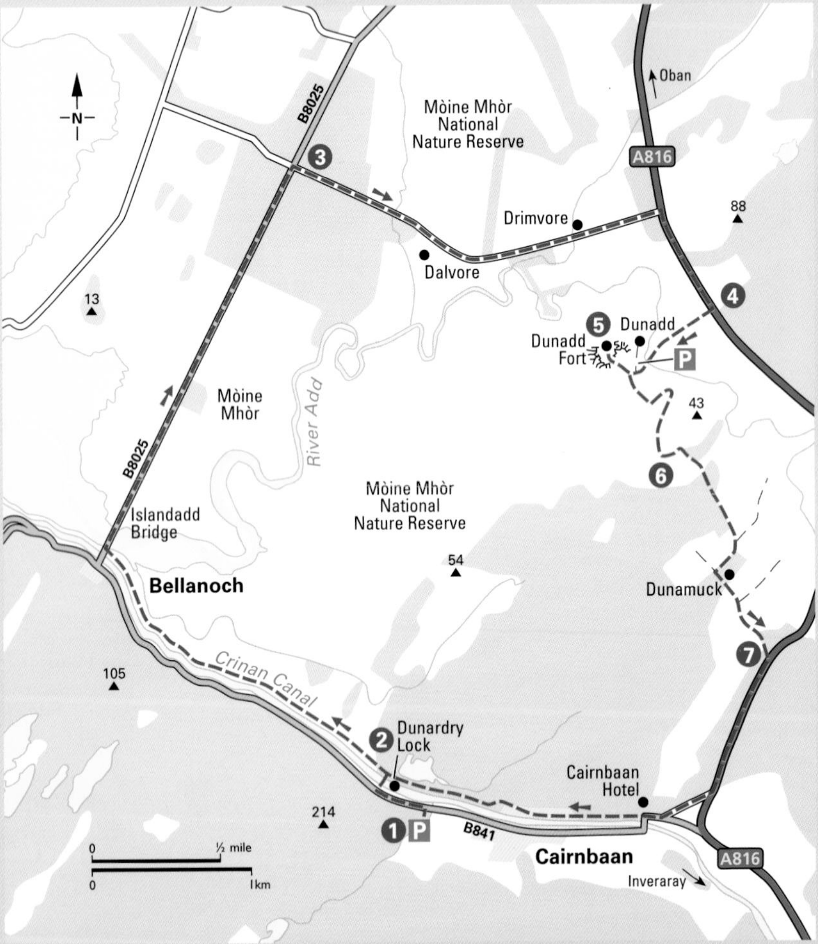

Route Directions

1 From the car park go down some steps, cross the road and turn left. Keep going until you reach a white cottage on your right. Turn right and on to a dirt track that runs behind the cottage, then go through a gap between the fence and a wall. Cross the canal over Dunardry Lock and then turn left following the tow path.

2 Head along the tow path as far as Bellanoch Bridge and then turn right on to the road, cross over Islandadd Bridge and on to the B8025. This narrow, but not busy, road is long and straight and runs right through the Mòine Mhór. Keep going ahead for nearly 2 miles (3.2km) then turn right on to an unclassified road, which is signposted for Drimvore.

3 Follow this for about 1.75 miles (2.8km) as it runs through the National Nature Reserve and passes the farms of Dalvore and Drimvore. Finally at a T-junction with the A816 turn right. After 0.5 mile (800m) an Historic Scotland fingerpost will point you in the direction of Dunadd Fort.

4 Turn right here on to a long straight farm road and keep on it, passing the farm of Dunadd, until you reach the Historic Scotland car park. Make your way towards the hill on a well-trodden path, go past the house on the left and through a kissing gate. Continue on the path, following the direction arrows, to emerge through a gap in some rocks within the outer ramparts.

5 Continue from here to the summit and after you have admired the views, seen the carvings and tried your own foot in the carved footprint, return by the same route to the car park. Leave it and turn right on to a farm track. Go through a gate then, almost immediately, go left through another gate and follow it as it curves left.

6 Another gate is encountered just before the road turns right and heads uphill. Continue following the road going through another gate until you reach the steading of Dunamuck farm. Turn left through the steading, go through a gate and then head downhill on a farm road, continuing along it until you reach a T-junction with the A816.

Route facts

DISTANCE/TIME 8.25 miles (13.3km) 5h

MAP OS Explorer 358 Lochgilphead & Knapdale North

START Dunardry Forest car park, grid ref: NR 824908

TRACKS Canal tow path, country roads and farm tracks

GETTING TO THE START From Lochgilphead take the A816 north to the junction with the B841. Turn left, following the Crinan Canal through Cairnbaan. The Dunardry Forest car park is on the left shortly after exiting the village.

THE PUB The Cairnbaan Hotel & Restaurant, Cairnbaan, by Lochgilphead. Tel: 01546 603668

7 Turn right on to the road and follow it for about 0.5 mile (800m), then turn right on to the road signposted for Cairnbaan and Crinan. After 0.25 mile (400m) turn right towards Crinan. As the road turns left across the swing bridge keep walking straight ahead and on to the canal tow path. Follow this back to Dunardry Lock and retrace your steps to the car park.

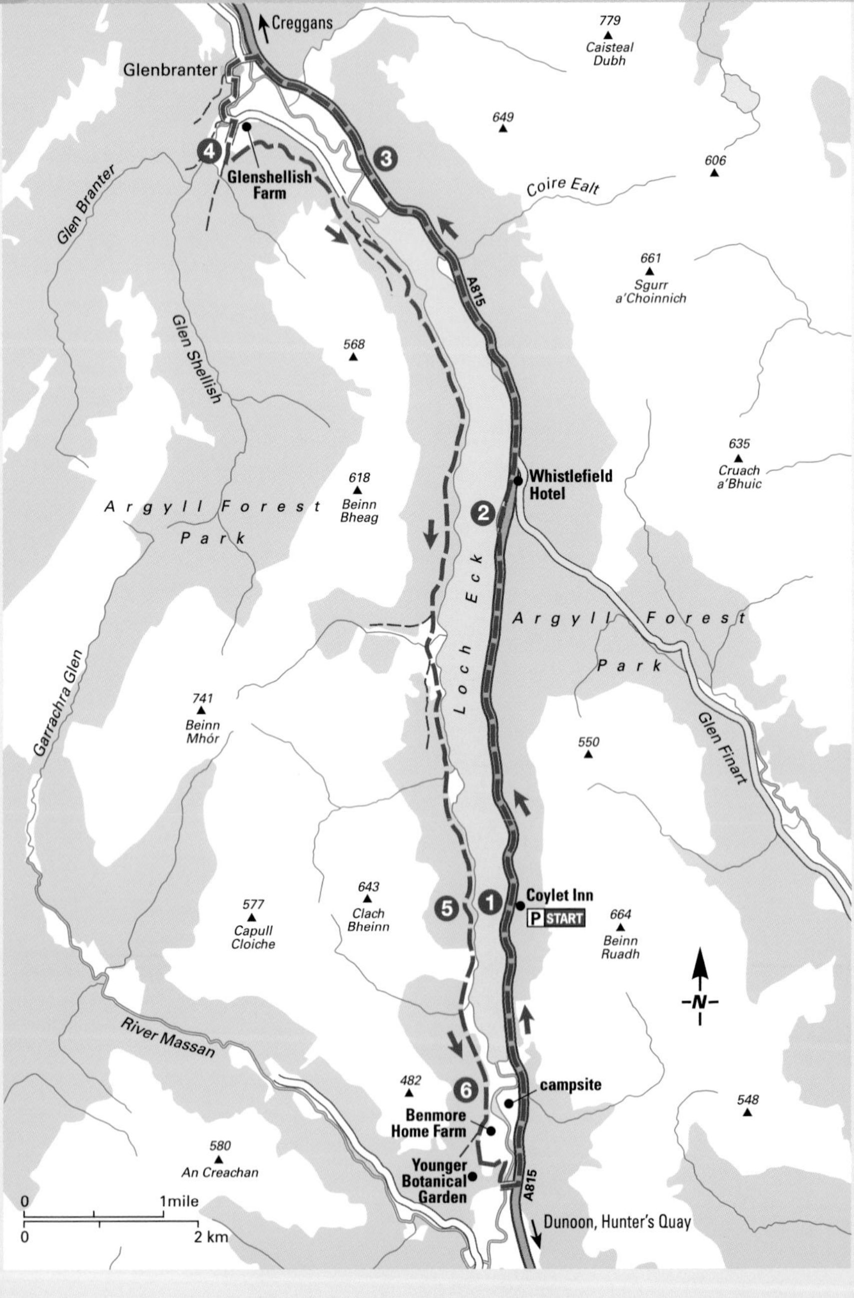
Creggans
779
Caisteal Dubh
Glenbranter
649
4
3
Glenshellish Farm
606
Glen Branter
Coire Ealt
661
Sgurr a'Choinnich
A815
568
Glen Shellish
635
Cruach a'Bhuic
618
Beinn Bheag
Whistlefield Hotel
2
Argyll Forest Park
Loch Eck
Argyll Forest Park
Glen Finart
Garrachra Glen
741
Beinn Mhór
550
643
Clach Bheinn
577
Capull Cloiche
5
1
Coylet Inn
P START
664
Beinn Ruadh
N
River Massan
482
6
campsite
548
Benmore Home Farm
580
An Creachan
Younger Botanical Garden
A815
0
1mile
0
2 km
Dunoon, Hunter's Quay

Argyll Forest Park

The Argyll Forest Park (parts of which belong to the larger Loch Lomond and Trossachs National Park) overflows with spectacular scenery, much of it forged during the ice age, with the long stretch of Loch Eck, a flurry of hills and forests, and the shadows of bigger Scottish peaks lurking in the background. This long, spectacular route skirts first along the banks of Loch Eck before climbing into the dense native Caledonian forest with sweeping views of the hills and the loch all around. Outdoor enthusiasts are well catered for here.

Route Directions

1 With your back to the loch leave the Coylet car park and turn left. Head north up the A815, a road with great loch views, but be aware of any traffic. Picnic sites dot this side of the loch allowing plenty of photo opportunities.

2 Come off the road to the left at the Rubha Croise picnic spot and take in the views. Cycle north past a gate on the old road (closed to vehicles), and continue to its end where it rejoins the A815 by the Whistlefield Hotel.

3 As the road continues past the loch along a flood plain, look out for the left turn to Glenbranter that leads over an old stone bridge. Follow the signs for the Forestry Commission office and then continue on the gravel track towards the loch. The track soon splits; take the left turn over the bridge towards Glenshellish Farm and then follow the blue/green cycle trail to the right.

4 A steep climb leads up through the forest before the track splits; follow the green route to the left and then keep following the white ringed trail posts that lead down to, and then along, the shores of Loch Eck.

5 When The Coylet Inn rears into view on the opposite bank of the loch there is a small beach that is ideal for a rest stop, with the waters of the loch lapping against the shingle and sand beach.

6 As the forest track becomes surfaced and then passes a campsite, look out for a left turn after Benmore Home Farm, which leads into the Younger Botanical Garden. Take the second bridge across the water and through their car park and you are back on the A815 with just a short stretch along the loch to cycle back to The Coylet Inn.

Route facts

DISTANCE/TIME 16 miles (25.5km) 3.5h

MAP OS Explorer 363 Cowal East

START The Coylet Inn (ask permission to park), grid ref: NS144887.

TRACKS road and solid forest tracks

GETTING TO THE START The Coylet Inn is on the A815, 9 miles (14.5km) north of Hunter's Quay on the Cowal Peninsula that is connected to the port of Gourock by a regular car and passenger ferry. Gourock itself is a 30-minute drive west of Glasgow.

CYCLE HIRE Hunter's Quay Holiday Village (10-minute drive from Loch Eck). Tel: 07795 301748

THE PUB The Coylet Inn, Lock Eck, Argyll. Tel: 01369 840426

❗ Take care on the A815, steep section on the start of the route back from the top of the loch. You can avoid this by cutting through Glenshellish Farm nearer the loch (left after crossing the bridge at Point 4).

GLASGOW MAP REF NS5966

Scotland's second city, Glasgow grew on the back of the tobacco trade with the New World to become one of the major industrial and engineering centres of Britain in the 19th century. In the 20th century its fortunes changed, as ship-building and manufacturing slumped after the Second World War. In recent years, however, it has reinvented itself as a vibrant and stylish place to be, making the most of its Victorian heritage of buildings, celebrating the designs of its most famous son, Charles Rennie Mackintosh (1868–1928), and investing in daring new projects that include the 'Armadillo' Scottish Exhibition and Conference Centre and the titanium-clad Science Centre. The trendy bars, cafés and restaurants spill out onto the pavements, and the city is known across the world for its classy shopping, with malls selling everything from top quality modern furniture to luxury chocolate, bold, cutting edge designer fashion, in addition to hand-crafted jewellery.

Glasgow is full of things to do and see. Highlights include the treasures on show in the popular Kelvingrove Museum, which includes a Mini-Museum for under-5s, and a section of hands-on exhibits; the fabulous Science Centre, with around 500 interactive exhibits to explain everything from the structure of the Forth Bridge to the movement of an artificial limb; and the People's Palace – the red-brick museum of local life on Glasgow Green which captures the wit, eccentricity and gritty character of the city, telling its history through familiar objects and quotes from real people.

South of the city centre, in leafy Pollok Park, is Glasgow's outstanding art collection, made by shipping magnate William Burrell, and displaying a small range of exquisite pieces – from original paintings to Chinese porcelain to some medieval tapestries and stained glass – in a small, purpose-built gallery. 'Musts' on the Mackintosh trail include Glasgow School of Art, the House for an Art Lover, the Mackintosh House at the university's Hunterian Museum, and the famous Willow Tearoom. The Kibble Palace, a vast Victorian glasshouse in the Botanic Gardens of the West End, is the perfect escape on a wet or chilly day.

GLEN COE & RANNOCH MOOR MAP REFS NN1058/NN3052

On 13 February 1692 the Campbells clan defied the age-old traditions of Highland hospitality and massacred 38 members of the Macdonald clan in Glen Coe. Alastair Macdonald, like many clansmen reluctant to accept William and Mary as ruling monarchs, failed to get papers attesting his loyalty to a magistrate by the deadline, the end of 1691, though they did arrive in Edinburgh in the new year. However, the papers were secretly suppressed by the Under Secretary of State, who then told Campbell of Glenlyon that the Macdonalds 'must all be slaughtered'. Campbell and his men, pretending to be delayed on a journey, were accommodated by the Macdonalds in Glen Coe for a fortnight, then cold-bloodedly slaughtered their hosts.

The atrocity took place in the lower glen by Glencoe village, where the now heather-roofed Folk Museum offers

PAP OF GLEN COE & LOCH LEVEN

Activity

GOING DOWNHILL FAST

Glen Coe's skiing may not be as fashionable as Klosters', but it can be just as exciting. From White Corries at the top of the glen, a chairlift takes skiers (and summer visitors) high into the mountains, where there are superb views to Rannoch Moor and beyond. There are 16 runs catering for all abilities, some with intriguing names – Fly Paper, for example, and Mug's Alley. Instruction is available. If hurtling downhill doesn't appeal, the Glen Coe area offers cross-country skiing, ski mountaineering, snowboarding, speed skating, and even paragliding.

displays of real Highland life. The most dramatic part of Glen Coe is higher up. From the roof of the National Trust for Scotland Visitor Centre there is a fine view of outstanding mountain scenery of stark peaks and glittering waterfalls. You can get details about the many exhilarating walks from the Visitor Centre; there is challenging climbing, too, for the experienced.

Southeast of Glen Coe, Rannoch Moor is a vast expanse of peat bog, treacherous even in the driest season. Rannoch actually means 'watery' in Gaelic. The finest view is perhaps from the railway as it crosses on its way north to Fort William, but the best approach by car is along Loch Rannoch. On its south side is the Black Wood of Rannoch, native Caledonian forest of ancient pines and groves of alder, birch and juniper. Just beyond Bridge of Gaur is a house built as barracks for Hanoverian troops after Culloden – a bleak posting. Rannoch Station is the end of the road, though it is possible to walk from here on old tracks. In places you will come across the blackened stumps of ancient trees protruding from the peat – this is evidence that this forlorn place was once covered in forest.

INVERARAY MAP REF NN0908

Inveraray, on the shores of Loch Fyne, is as fine an example of town planning as you will find, created by the 3rd Duke of Argyll in the 1740s to sit at the gates of his grand new home. It seems a great deal of trouble to go to, just to move your ancestral home by 0.5 mile (800m), but this was, after all, the extravagant 18th century. The little town that the Duke created is stylish, with a wide main street of white-painted houses running up to the classical kirk. Down at the waterfront are brilliant white arches, one of which leads up to All Saints Episcopal Church – climb the bell-tower for a wonderful panoramic view of the town, the castle, the loch and the hills.

Inveraray Castle, now home to the 13th Duke and his family, is a neo-Gothic building with pointed sash windows and battlements. Inside, its most spectacular feature is the Armoury Hall, the tallest room in Scotland, which is dramatically adorned with pikes, axes, swords and muskets. A walking tour of the castle includes splendid state rooms with ornate gilded plasterwork, fine furniture and Campbell family portraits.

Moored on the loch side is the three-masted vessel *Arctic Penguin*, upon which you can take a turn at steering, ring the ship's telegraph, visit the engine room and watch archive film of old sailing and steam ships. Inveraray Jail, near the kirk, has opened its doors to willing visitors. In the semi-circular courtroom you can be part of the crowd hearing a trial, and in the 19th-century cells you can try out canvas hammocks and turn the crank machine. You can even see mug-shots of petty criminals.

KILMARTIN MAP REF NR8398

The waters of Loch Awe once flowed southwards through the glacier-formed Kilmartin Glen, depositing sediment on the valley floor. The area was occupied by farmers from early prehistoric times, and the concentration of monuments that they left behind makes this one of the richest archaeological areas in Scotland. At Achnabreck is the largest group of cup-and-ring marked rocks in Britain, but even more impressive remains are to be found further north.

The tall, flat-faced Ballymeanoch standing stones and a line of burial cairns stretch towards Kilmartin village. Ri Cruin is a crescent of boulders in a grove, and carvings of axeheads and, possibly, a boat's keel can be seen on the stones. The three Nether Largie cairns are higher – especially the most southerly, with its large chamber topped by huge stone slabs. Central to the site is Temple Wood Circle, begun around 3000 BC and modified several times up to 1200 BC. To get the most out of this fascinating area head over to the superb interpretative museum in Kilmartin village, where there is also an extensive collection of carved 9th- to 16th-century grave slabs in the churchyard.

Carnasserie Castle, further up the valley, is a well-preserved fortified house from the 16th century.

KINTYRE MAP REF NR8768

At the north end of Kintyre and 38 miles (61km) from Campbeltown, the pretty fishing port of Tarbert has rows of colour-washed houses and the remains of a 15th-century tower house built on the site of a former royal castle. The Campbeltown road follows the wind-swept west fringe of Kintyre, with wide views over to Jura and Islay, and then the hills give way to a gentler landscape towards the handsome harbour of Campbeltown. By the waterfront is the 15th-century Campbeltown Cross, and near by is an unexpected delight – the 1913 art deco front of the 256-seat Picture House. Davaar Island, reached on foot at low tide, shelters the harbour, and on its south side is a restored cave-painting of the crucifixion, originally created by Archibald MacKinnon in 1887.

Visit

DALRIADA

From around AD 500 the Scottish kingdom of Dalriada had its capital in the hill fort at Dunadd. There are traces of buildings on the hillside and defensive terraces around the summit. Carved in the rock a little way outside is an inscription in Ogham script – evidence of Pictish use of the hilltop – as well as a basin and a footprint that may have been used at coronations. Some people believe that Aidan was crowned first Christian king in Britain here in AD 574 by St Columba, and that the stone used became the Stone of Scone, once in Westminster Abbey but now safe and on display in Edinburgh Castle.

St Columba landed near Southend at the foot of the peninsula – a ruined chapel and two footprints carved in a nearby rock mark the spot. A winding road eastwards goes to the Mull of Kintyre, with its lighthouse – a stark, windswept place, only 12 miles (19.5km) from Ireland. A single-track, hairpin road with breathtaking views over Arran follows the western coast back to Campbeltown; alternatively retrace your route up the B842, diverting west to the superb sands of Machrihanish, where the golf course is on the bay's edge.

To the north of Campbeltown, the east coast route is slow and winding, with tree-lined glens and fertile valleys. Up the valley from the battlemented castle by the shore at Saddell (now let by the Landmark Trust) are the remains of Saddell Abbey, with its impressive collection of carved gravestones (open access). Carradale, further up the coast, is a small rural village beside a beautiful sandy bay. You can catch the summer ferry from Claonaig to Lochranza on Arran, and at Skipness you can explore the fine castle ruins or wander around the 13th-century Kilbrannan Chapel.

LOCHGILPHEAD MAP REF NR8688

Lochgilphead was once the centre of herring fishing on Loch Gilp, with a wooden pier stretched across the bay, but the fish mysteriously vanished before the First World War. Mills and dyeworks also disappeared, and, besides tourism centred around the Crinan Canal, the main employer is now Argyll and Bute Council, which has its headquarters at Kilmory Castle.

The castle gardens, now open to the public, were partly laid out by Joseph Hooker, first director of Kew Gardens. They are full of rare rhododendrons, as is Crarae Garden, on the Inveraray road, which is planted round a spectacular gorge. A little further to the north is Auchindrain township, a former crofting settlement which now gives visitors an experience of Highland life. Its houses have original furniture and the barns are equipped with old implements.

Glacial action reversed the waters of Loch Awe, to the north of Lochgilphead, to flow through the dramatic Pass of Brander instead of through Kilmartin Glen. The longest loch in Scotland – measuring nearly 25 miles (40km), more than a mile (1.6km) longer than Loch Ness – it is very narrow, and the north end is dominated by the peak of Ben Cruachan. You can take a steamboat trip from Lochawe village which includes the impressive ruins of Kilchurn Castle. Ardanaiseig Gardens, surrounding a beautiful old hotel and beside the western shore of the loch, are full of glowing rhododendrons and specimen trees. It is worth following the minor road south through Inverliever Forest, which offers many forest walks and some spectacular high viewpoints over the loch. The eastern shore road gives views of the loch's small islands, some with ancient chapels and burial grounds.

LOCH LOMOND MAP REF NS3889

Part of Scotland's first National Park (Loch Lomond and the Trossachs National Park was established in 2002), Loch Lomond has two very distinct

Visit

MOUNTAIN POWER

Ben Cruachan holds a secret – Scotland's first big pump storage power station. The Visitor Centre explains how water from an artificial loch high up on the mountain is fed down through the rock to turbines within the mountain. Off-peak power is used to pump the water back up to the reservoir. The highlight of any visit is a 0.75-mile (1.2km) ride down tunnels to the huge turbine hall, 300 feet (91.5m) long and 120 feet (36.5m) high. The plants along the way are real – tropical species, which are thriving happily in the artificial light, heat and humidity of the tunnels.

characters – the narrow upper loch is hemmed in by mountains, and stretches up into the heart of the Highlands, while the broad, island-speckled southern end is bordered by fertile farmland. Here, within easy reach of Glasgow, are some of the loch's most popular attractions.

Balloch, with its modern castle, country park and opportunities for boat cruises, sits astride the only natural outlet from the loch, and is a popular centre. The Loch Lomond Shores Visitor Centre includes an information centre and shopping outlets. Up the west side, off the well-used A82, is Luss, a smart estate village which was the setting for the television series, *Take the High Road*.

Lomond's east side is much quieter, offering walking and outdoor pursuits. From Balmaha there are some good views over several of the loch's 38 named islands – especially Inchcailloch, once the site of a nunnery, and now part of the Loch Lomond National Nature Reserve. Much of the eastern shore is within the 50,000-acre (20,000ha) Queen Elizabeth Forest Park. The narrow road ends at Rowardennan, from where there is a stiff climb up the 3,192 feet (973m) of Ben Lomond. To visit the beautiful Inversnaid, approach from Aberfoyle or by ferry from Inveruglas – unless you are energetic enough for the walk along the West Highland Way from Rowardennan.

It is on the shores of Loch Lomond that the 95-mile (153km) West Highland Way, Scotland's first long-distance footpath, makes the transition from easy lowland walking to the more rugged terrain of the Highlands. Starting from Milngavie (pronounced Mull-guy) on the outskirts of Glasgow, the route makes its way north to Fort William, often using ancient and historic routes – drove roads by which cattle dealers reached market (like the Devil's Staircase out of Glen Coe), military roads instituted by General Wade to aid in suppressing the clans, old coaching roads and even discarded railway lines. Walk all the way if you wish – experts recommend going south to north, to build up stamina for the hills – or take a short walk along the route; there is no shortage of breathtaking sections, and you may see red deer and, just possibly, golden eagles on the way.

MULL & IONA

MAP REF NM7273

Take the time to properly explore and discover Mull and you will find it full of interest and beauty. Craignure is the main arrival point, and from Old Pier Station the Mull and West Highland Narrow Gauge Railway runs the extremely scenic 1.25 miles (2km) to Torosay Castle. This line boasts a real rarity – a modern steam locomotive, built in Sheffield in 1993.

Torosay Castle is actually a Victorian mansion, set in 12 acres (5ha) of superb gardens. The house is full of character and is enthusiastically shared with all visitors by its resident owner – you are positively encouraged to sit on chairs, peer into cupboards and browse through the family scrapbooks. Near by, on a craggy point with wonderful views along the Sound of Mull, is 13th-century Duart Castle, centre for the Clan Maclean.

Mountains give way to pretty pastoral scenery on the way to the little island's capital, Tobermory, with its houses painted in jolly colours around the bay – a familiar sight to fans of TV's *Balamory* for young children. Tobermory's tourist attractions – the Mull Museum and the distillery – are tiny. Calgary, further on, has an interesting sculpture trail and the best sandy beach on the island.

West of Ben More, Mull's highest mountain, is the Ardmeanach peninsula, the tip of which is only accessible by an arduous 5.5-mile (8.8km) path. Its main sight is MacCulloch's Tree, 50 feet (15m) high and engulfed in lava more than 50 million years ago. Boat trips round Mull sometimes give passengers a view of it.

Mull's main road is mostly single track and traverses the moorland from the east coast to Loch Scridain, and on across the Ross of Mull to Fionnphort, for the Iona ferry. South of the road is fine walking country, with a coastline of basalt stacks and sea arches – wild and lonely, and full of fascinating wildlife.

Iona is a magical place. Most visitors make straight for the abbey, but you should spare time for the remains of the 13th-century priory, built for the use of Augustinian nuns. St Columba founded his monastery in AD 563 where the abbey now stands, and from it the teachings of Christianity radiated throughout Europe. The monks compiled a library of illuminated manuscripts including the Book of Kells, now on show in Dublin's Trinity College Library. Columba's foundation ended in AD 806 when Vikings slew 68 monks at Martyrs' Bay. Later a church and buildings erected there by 12th-century Benedictine monks were left in ruins after the Reformation, until restoration began in 1910. Currently the home of the Iona Community, founded in 1938, the abbey welcomes pilgrims from around the world. Right beside it is the ancient burial ground of the Scottish kings, among them notably Macbeth and Duncan. The abbey does get busy with visitors at times, but although the island is small, it is possible to escape the crowds quickly and enjoy the fine sands and rocky landscape, the wild flowers and birds, and far-reaching sea views.

Many visitors will know of Staffa because of composer Mendelssohn's 'Fingal's Cave' overture. He came to this extraordinary island in 1829, to visit the cavern on its south side. Here, the dark volcanic basalt has cooled and formed its characteristic six-sided columns, making it look like a massive cathedral organ. The enormous interior of Fingal's Cave is also like a cathedral; weather permitting, visitors can land from some of the boat trips in the area.

The Carbeth Hut Community

A short walk in the shadow of the Campsie Hills, to discover the Carbeth hut community established after World War I by the unemployed seeking an escape into the countryside. The first hut was built in 1919 and by the 1930s there were more than 30 dwellings. Their ingenious and often ramshackle homes were constructed from any materials that were available free of charge or for little money. Conditions were spartan but met the needs of the people and were probably as good as they had at home. During the summers, the area round the Carbeth Inn was alive with activity as whole families decamped to the countryside for their holidays.

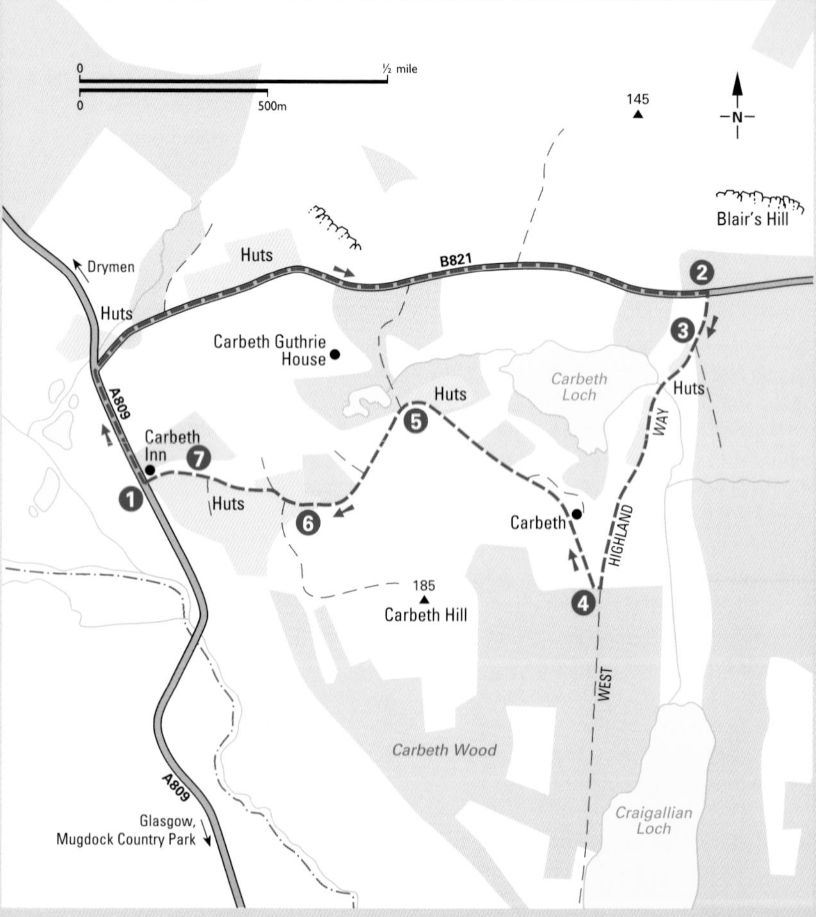

Route Directions

1 From the car park at the Carbeth Inn turn right on to the A809. After 0.25 mile (400m) take the first turning right on to the B821. Continue ahead on this road for a mile (1.6km), passing a collection of huts on the left and ignoring a public footpath sign to the right.

2 Turn right at the signpost for the West Highland Way. There's also a Scottish Rights of Way Society signpost beside this pointing to the Khyber Pass Road to Mugdock Country Park. This was the favoured route of the early walkers heading out of Glasgow to the Campsie Fells and beyond.

3 Go through a gate and continue along a well-surfaced access road. Ignoring the Khyber Pass turn-off, keep right to follow the West Highland Way along the access road to more huts. After passing the first of the huts and reaching a left bend in the path, look out for a partially concealed public path signpost on the right beside a West Highland Way marker post.

4 Turn right here on to a narrow but well-surfaced footpath and continue along it, passing Carbeth Loch on the right-hand side, to reach the junction with the drive leading to Carbeth House. This is a private house and is not open to the public. Turn left, pass a house and some huts on the right then take the next turning on the left.

5 Continue along this lane, then head uphill to reach another grouping of the Carbeth huts. Follow the main route through the huts and when it forks, keep left.

6 Keep on this road as it passes through the main part of the Carbeth huts, an extraordinary assortment of small dwellings, shanties and shacks. Ignore all of the smaller tracks branching off this road. They allow access to individual huts or other parts of the settlement.

7 Eventually reach a T-junction. Turn right and follow the lane as it winds downhill to reach the junction with the A809 beside the Carbeth Inn. Turn left and return to the car park.

Route facts

DISTANCE/TIME 3 miles (4.8km) 2h30

MAP OS Explorer 348 Campsie Fells

START The Carbeth Inn (check beforehand with landlord if you wish to park here), grid ref: NX 524791

TRACKS Roads, access tracks and footpaths, 1 stile

GETTING TO THE START
The Carbeth Inn is on the A809, approximately 10 miles (16.1km)north of Glasgow. Follow the road out of the city and past a golf course. Shortly after crossing Allander Water the Inn is on your right-hand side.

THE PUB The Carbeth Inn, Blanefield.
Tel: 01360 770002

Insight

SPANISH TREASURE

There is an old treasure map, now on display at Inveraray Castle, showing the location of the wreck of a Spanish galleon that sank in Tobermory Bay in 1588. After the defeat of the Armada, many Spaniards attempted to get home via the north of Scotland. The legend goes that one such vessel was given supplies by the people of Mull, but the Spanish refused to pay, and even locked up Donald Maclean, who had come to collect the payment. He managed to escape, and blew up the ship, which sank in the bay. Confusion reigns as to whether the ship was a troop carrier, the *San Juan de Sicilia*, or a treasure ship, the *Florida*. Another theory is that the English sent agents who destroyed the vessel. Treasure hunters are ever hopeful, and still dive here in search of a shower of golden ducats, yet so far only a few coins and cannon have been raised.

Insight

FERRY CONVENIENT

You can't get far in Western Scotland without needing to catch a ferry, especially to its 130 or so inhabited islands. Many of the shorter routes are operated by local owners and provide an excellent service, but Caledonian MacBrayne – CalMac – is undoubtedly the name you will come across most. The company was formed in 1973 when MacBraynes, operators of shipping services mostly to the Western Isles since 1851, joined forces with the Clyde-based Caledonian Steam Packet Company, founded in 1889. CalMac sails to 22 islands and operates more than 29 ferries in a huge range of sizes, from the largest vessels working the Ullapool to Stornoway route, capable of taking 690 passengers and 123 cars, to the six-car ferries that ply from Oban to Lismore. Carrying 4.5 million passengers each year, it even has its own Facebook fan base.

OBAN MAP REF NM8629

To experience the true splendour of Oban, you should climb at dusk to MacCaig's improbable Gothic Coliseum and watch the glorious sunset over the Firth of Lorne and the mountains of Morvern and Mull. MacCaig engaged unemployed stonemasons on his spectacular tower from around 1897, and though it was never finished, it is Oban's most notable landmark. At its foot, the bay, sheltered by the island of Kerrera, is busy with pleasure craft.

Much of the broad harbour front is dominated by hotels, and ferries for the Hebrides depart from Railway Quay. The modest War and Peace Museum, in the old newspaper offices of the *Oban Times*, offers an insight into the town during the war years when flying boats operated from here, and other local history.

Oban Distillery, set in the heart of the town, welcomes visitors, and near by you'll find Geoffrey (Tailor) making kilts.

Northwards, the soaring tower of St Columba's Cathedral dominates the bay, and beyond it are the haunting remains of Dunollie Castle. A few miles further on, Dunstaffnage Castle, a mostly ruined stronghold with gatehouse, two round towers and 10-foot (3m) thick walls, stands on a rocky outcrop, and was once the prison of Flora Macdonald.

Across the Connel Bridge in the little town of Barcaldine is the Scottish Sea Life Sanctuary, where you can see British marine life, including rescued common and grey seals, at close quarters. From here, drive to Arduaine Garden with its superb rhododendrons and wonderful views to the Isle of Jura.

PLACES OF INTEREST

Ardkinglas Woodland Garden
Cairndow, Loch Fyne.
Tel: 01499 600261;
www.ardkinglas.com

Ardnamurchan Lighthouse Visitor Centre
Ardnamurchan Point,
west of Fort William.
Tel: 01972 510210

Arduaine Garden (NTS)
20 miles (32km) south of
Oban, on A816.
Tel: 044 493 2216

Auchindrain Air Museum
On A83, south of Inveraray.
Tel: 01499 500235; www.
auchindrain-museum.org.uk

Balloch Castle Country Park
Balloch.
Tel: 01389 722600

Benmore Botanic Garden
7 miles (11.3km) north of
Dunoon on A815.
Tel: 01369 706261;
www.rbge.org.uk

Bonawe Iron Furnace (HS)
Taynuilt. Tel: 01866 822432

Botanic Gardens
Great Western Road,
Glasgow. Tel: 0141 276 1614;
www.glasgow.gov.uk

Brodick Castle, Garden & Country Park (NTS)
Brodick, Isle of Arran.
Tel: 0844 493 2152

Burrell Collection
Pollok Country Park,
Glasgow. Tel: 0141 287 2550;
www.glasgowmuseums.com

Carnasserie Castle (HS)
2 miles (3.2km) north of
Kilmartin, off A816.

Crarae Garden
Crarae, 10 miles (16.1km)
south of Inveraray.
Tel: 0844 493 2210

Cruachan Power Station Visitor Centre
Dalmally. Tel: 01866 822618;
www.visitcruachan.co.uk

Duart Castle
South of Craignure, Isle of
Mull, off A849.
Tel: 01680 812309;
www.duartcastle.com

Dunadd Fort (HS)
Kilmartin Glen.

Dunstaffnage Castle
4 miles (6.4km) north of
Oban, off A85.
Tel: 01631 562465

Glasgow School of Art
167 Renfrew Street,
Glasgow.
Tel: 0141 353 4500;
www.gsa.ac.uk

Glencoe & North Lorn Folk Museum
Glencoe, Ballaculish.
Tel: 01855 811664

Glencoe Visitor Centre (NTS)
Glencoe. Tel: 0844 493 2222

House for an Art Lover
Bellahouston Park,
10 Dumbreck Road,
Glasgow. Tel: 0141 353 4770;
www.houseforanartlover.
co.uk

Inveraray Castle
Inveraray. Tel: 01499 302203;
www.inveraray-castle.com

Isle of Arran Distillery Visitor Centre
Lochranza, Arran.
Tel: 01770 830264;
www.arranwhisky.com.

Kelvingrove Art Gallery & Museum
Argyle Street, Glasgow.
Tel: 0141 276 9599; www.
glasgowmuseums.com.

Kilchurn Castle (HS)
Loch Awe.

Kilmartin House Museum
Kilmartin. Tel: 01546 510278;
www.kilmartin.org

Kilmory Castle Gardens
Lochgilphead.
Tel: 01546 602127;
www.argyll-bute.gov.uk

Mount Stewart House
Rothesay, Bute.
Tel: 01700 503877;
www.mountstewart.com

Mull Museum
Main Street, Tobermory, Mull.
Tel: 01688 301100;
www.mullmuseum.org.uk

Oban Distillery
Stafford Street, Oban.
Tel: 01631 572004

Oban War and Peace Museum
Old Oban Times Building,
Corran Esplanade, Oban.
Tel: 01631 570007;
www.obanmuseum.org.uk

People's Palace
Glasgow Green, Glasgow.
Tel: 0141 276 0788; www.
glasgowmuseums.com

Rothesay Castle (HS)
Castlehill Street, Rothesay, Bute. Tel: 01700 502691

Torosay Castle and Gardens
Mull. One mile (1.6km) south of Craignure.
Tel: 01680 812421

FOR CHILDREN

Inveraray Maritime Experience
The Pier, Inveraray.
Tel: 01499 302213;
www.inverarаypier.com

Glasgow Science Centre
50 Pacific Quay, Glasgow.
Tel: 0141 420 5000; www.glasgowsciencecentre.org.uk

Inveraray Jail
Church Square, Inveraray.
Tel: 01499 302381;
www.inverarayjail.co.uk

Scottish Sea Life Sanctuary
Off A828, on shore of Loch Creran, Barcaldine.
Tel: 01631 720386;
www.sealsanctuary.co.uk

SHOPPING

Arran Fine Foods
The Old Mill, Lamlash, Arran.
Tel: 01506 431031;
www.paterson-arran.com

Creelers Smokehouse
Home Farm, Brodick, Arran.
Tel: 01770 302797;
www.creelers.co.uk

Dunoon Ceramics
Pot Shop, 162 Argyll Street, Dunoon.
Tel: 01369 702662

Geoffrey (Tailor) Kiltmakers & Weavers
35 Stevenson Street, Oban.
Tel: 01631 570557;
www.geoffreykilts.co.uk

Inverawe Smokehouses Visitor Centre
Taynuilt.
Tel: 0844 847 5490; www.smoked-salmon.co.uk

Island Cheese Company
Home Farm, Brodick, Arran.
Tel: 01770 302788;
www.islandcheese.co.uk

Loch Fyne Oyster Bar & Seafood Shop
Cairndow.
Tel: 01499 600236;
www.lochfyne.com

Loch Lomond Shores
Ben Lomond Way, Balloch.
Tel: 01389 751035;
www.lochlomondshores.com

Tiso Glasgow Outdoor Experience
50 Couper Street, Glasgow.
Tel: 0141 559 5450;
www.tiso.com

SPORTS & ACTIVITIES

ADVENTURE SPORTS

Puffin Dive Centre
Port Gallanach, south of Oban.
Tel: 01631 555088;
www.puffin.org.uk

Quadmania Ltd
Stronchullin Farm, Blairmore, Dunoon.
Tel: 01369 810289; www.quadmaniascotland.co.uk

Lomond Adventure Canoe Hire
Balmaha House, Balmaha.
Tel: 01360 870218; www.lomandadventure.co.uk

Stramash Adventure Activities
Upper Soroba, Oban
Tel: 01631 566080
www.stramash.eu

BOAT TRIPS

Cruise Loch Lomond Ltd
The Boat Yard, Tarbet, Loch Lomond.
Tel: 01301 702356; www.cruiselochlomondltd.com

Loch Etive Cruises
Etive View, Taynuilt.
Tel: 01866 822430

Macfarlane & Son
The Boatyard, Balmaha.
Tel: 01360 870214;
www.balmahaboatyard.co.uk

Waverley Excursions Ltd
33 Lancefield Quay, Glasgow.
Tel: 0845 1304647; www.waverleyexcursions.co.uk

CYCLING

Crinan Cycles
Canal Basin Yard, Ardrishaig.
Tel: 01546 603511

Brown's Tobermory
21 Main Street, Tobermory, Mull. Tel: 01688 302020;
www.brownstobermory.co.uk

GOLF

Cowal Golf Club
Dunoon, off A815 at Kirn.
Tel: 01369 705673;
www.cowalgolfclub.com
18-hole course.

Craignure Golf Club
Scallastle, Craignure, Mull. Tel: 01680 300420; www.craignuregoldclub.co.uk
9-hole course.

Kyles of Bute Golf Club
The Moss, Kames, Tighnabruaich. Tel: 01700 811603
9-hole course.

Loch Lomond Golf Club
Rossdhu House, Luss. Tel: 01436 655555; www.lochlomond.com
18-hole course.

Machrihanish Golf Club
Machrihanish, north of Campbelltown. Tel: 01586 810213; www.machgolf.com
18-hole course.

Tobermory Golf Club
Erray Road, Tobermory, Mull. Tel: 01688 302741; www.tobermoraygolfclub.com
9-hole course.

HORSE-RIDING

Appaloosa Holidays, Lunga Riding Stables
Craobh Haven, by Lochgilphead. Tel: 01852 500632

Argyll Adventure
Dalchenna, Inveraray. Tel: 01499 302611; www.horserides.com

Argyll Trail Riding & Castle Riding Centre
Brenfield Farm, Ardrishaig. Tel: 01546 603274; www.brenfield.co.uk

LONG-DISTANCE FOOTPATHS

Cowal Way
Partially way-marked trail on Cowal Peninsula, 57 miles (92km). www.cowalway.org

Isle of Arran Coastal Way
Circular route, 65 miles (104km). www.coastalway.co.uk

Kintyre Way
New footpath runs from Tarbert to Southend, 89 miles (143km). www.kintyreway.com

West Highland Way
Scotland's most famous long-distance trail, Glasgow to Fort William, 96 miles (154km). www.west-highland-way.co.uk

WILDLIFE TOURS

Discover Mull
Ardrioch Farm, Dervaig, Mull. Tel: 01688 400415; www.discovermull.co.uk

Island Encounter
Arla Tir, Aros, Mull. Tel: 01680 300441; www.mullwildlife.co.uk

Sea.fari Adventures Oban
Easdale Harbour, Seil, by Oban. Tel: 01852 300003; www.seafari.co.uk. Wildlife safaris in rigid inflatables.

Turus Mara
Penmore Mill, Dervaig, Mull. Tel: 01688 400242; www.turusmara.com. Cruise tours from Ulva Ferry, Mull, or Oban, to Treshnish Isles, Staffa and Iona.

WINTER SPORTS

Glencoe Ski Centre
Kingshouse, Glencoe. Tel: 01855 851226; www.glencoemountain.co.uk

The Ice Factor
Leven Road, Kinlochleven. Tel: 01855 831100; www.ice-factor.co.uk

EVENTS & CUSTOMS

Balloch
Loch Lomond Highland Games, Jul

Dunoon
Cowal Highland Gathering, late Aug

Glasgow
Celtic Connections, folk music festival, Jan
International Jazz Festival, Jun
World Pipe Band Championships, mid-Aug

Inveraray
Highland Games, mid-Jul

Oban
Kilmore and Kilbride Highland Games, Jul
Argyllshire Highland Gathering, late Aug

Taynuilt
Taynuilt Highland Games, mid-Jul

Tobermory, Mull
Mull Music Festival, mid-Apr
Isle of Mull Car Rally, mid-Oct

Tea Rooms

The Coach House Coffee Shop

Loch Lomond Trading Co Ltd, Luss G83 8NN
Tel: 01436 860341; www.lochlomondtrading.com

Gaelic music, log fires and a kilted proprietor set the scene at this friendly coffee and gift shop in the pretty village of Luss, on Loch Lomond's western shore. The perfect spot for a light meal or tea stop, it offers home-made rolls and soup, and speciality fruit cake, laced with malt whisky or baked with ale and studded with crystallised ginger.

Castle Stalker View Café

Appin, Portnacroish, Argyll
Tel: 01631 730444; www.castlestalkerview.co.uk

Offering superb views down over the romantic ruin of Castle Stalker, this bright, modern west-coast tea room is the perfect place to pause for refreshment. Coffee and tea can be supplemented with freshly baked, cream-filled scones or tasty wedges of cake. Light lunches are available too, from soup and filled rolls to smoked salmon and haggis. Sit outside for the panoramic views on a sunny day.

The Willow Tearoom

217 Sauchiehall Street, Glasgow G2 3EX
Tel: 0141 332 0521; www.willowtearooms.co.uk

Above a jewellery shop, this is one of Kate Cranston's original tea rooms, designed by Charles Rennie Mackintosh in 1903. Sip your tea or coffee and tuck into delicious cakes, sandwiches and scones in the elegant Room de Luxe, with its wall-panelling, stylish stained glass and distinctive silver chairs.

Pubs

Cairnbaan Hotel & Restaurant

Cairnbaan, by Lochgilphead PA31 8SJ
Tel: 01546 603668

At this former 18th-century coaching inn, lighter meals are served in the lounge bar and conservatory, with lots of seafood but other choices too, such as chicken stuffed with haggis.

Crinan Hotel

Crinan, Argyll & Bute, PA31 8SR
Tel: 01546 830261; www.crinanhotel.com

The hotel is set by the little harbour, basin and lock at the end of the Crinan Canal, and offers the choice of the bar or restaurant. In both the seafood is excellent, offering such delights as a warm tart of local scallops with smoked bacon and juicy sun-dried tomatoes, or perhaps Loch Crinan seafood chowder.

The Inn at Inverbeg

Luss, by Loch Lomond G83 8PD
Tel: 01436 860678; www.inverbeghotel.co.uk

Recently refurbished as Scotland's first boutique inn, this was chosen as the AA's Pub of the Year for 2009–10. The views across Loch Lomond are breathtaking, and the food in Mr C's relaxed and informal dining room, based around fresh fish, is excellent. Choose from over 200 malts in the Whisky Bar.

Pierhouse Hotel & Restaurant

Port Appin, Argyll & Bute PA38 4DE
Tel: 01631 730302

A whitewashed hotel, with views towards Mull, that pays tribute to the skills of local fishermen, serving simply prepared fresh lobster, langoustines, mussels and salmon. There is an extensive wine list to match. Alternatives are chicken, venison and beef dishes, and food is served outdoors on sunny days.

GRANTOWN-ON-SPEY

Cairngorms & Central Highlands

INTRODUCTION

The area of Scotland's central Highlands includes some of the highest ground in Britain: the Cairngorm mountains, where its special ecological status is protected as a national park. Two of Scotland's greatest salmon rivers flow through here too, the mighty Spey and the Dee, and this has long been a popular sporting area, especially for climbing, walking and fishing. Now, outdoor activities are focused around Aviemore and the Spey valley, with layers of history to discover in the gentler lands to the north. Shaped by thousands of years of glacial ice, this brooding landscape is home to some of Scotland's most stunning birds, including golden eagles that nest on the mountain tops, and rare capercaillies that forage amid clumps of ancient woodland that clothe the hills.

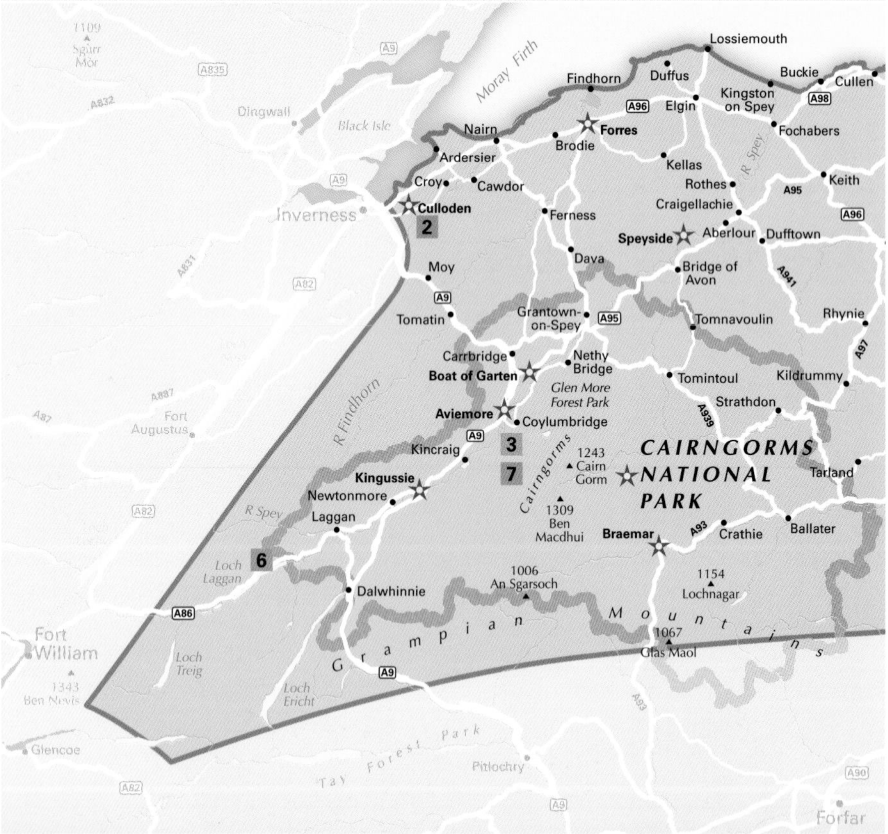

RIVER DEE

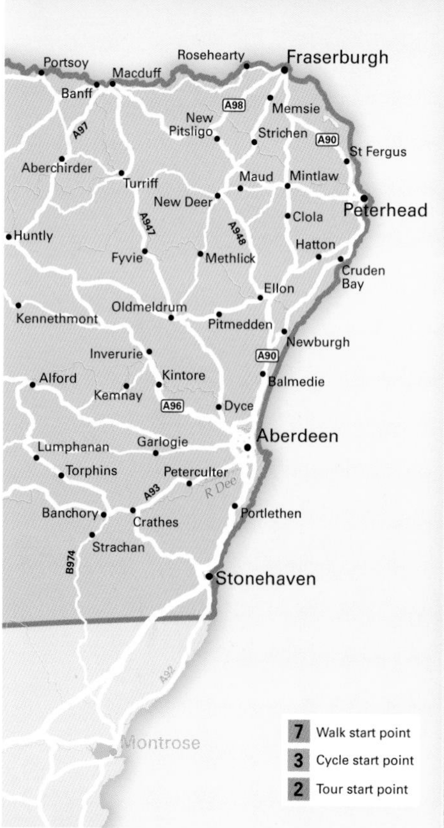

RED SQUIRREL, CAIRNGORMS NATIONAL PARK

Unmissable attractions

Attend the Braemar Gathering, the most famous Highland games in the world, to see, among others, tossing the caber and throwing the hammer competitions...tread the haunting ground where Bonnie Prince Charlie took on the might of the English army in the bloody Battle of Culloden...drive through the wooded Highland Wildlife Park where you can see herds of red deer and even bison from the comfort of your car...ski or snowboard down the snow-clad slopes at Aviemore, Scotland's premier winter sports venue...visit Forres, a place of condemned witches and fairy legends.

1 **Ruthven Barracks** The barracks were built just south of Kingussie to subdue Jacobite rebellion.

2 **Craigellachie Bridge** Thomas Telford built this bridge over the Spey, near Elgin, in 1814.

3 **The Cairngroms** Hikers enjoy the largest mountainscape in the UK.

4 **Crathes Castle Garden** The well-maintained castle is surrounded by wonderful gardens.

5 **Culloden Moor** A memorial to the brave Highlanders who fell in the fierce battle here.

6 **River Spey** A peaceful place to fish for salmon and sea trout.

7 **Strathspey Steam Railway** The railway is based at Aviemore in the Highlands.

4

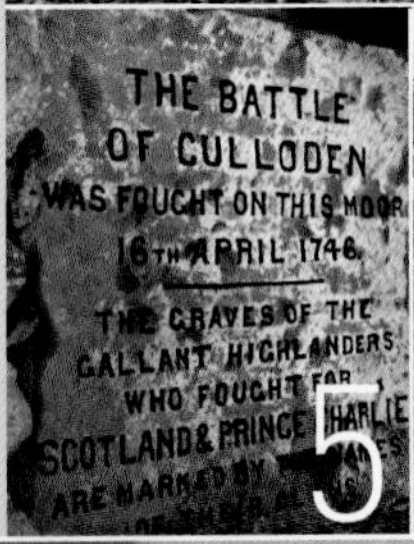

5

6

7

AVIEMORE MAP REF NH8913

The once-sleepy, remote railway station settlement of Aviemore was developed in the 1960s as a ski destination, and while it has never been able to rival the brash attractions of the Continental resorts, it manages to hold its own as an activities centre for the Cairngorms National Park. Its arcaded main street is a hang-over from an earlier time, but there is now a good range of outdoor shops and places to eat and relax.

The Rothiemurchus Estate, 1.5 miles (2.4km) to the south, has belonged to the Grant family since the 16th century. Elizabeth Grant's very readable account of her early life there, *Memoirs of a Highland Lady*, gives a captivating insight into the workings of the land here some 200 years ago, when timber was sawn by hand and floated down the Spey, and the idea of sustainable forestry was in barely its infancy.

Today the estate offers an amazing variety of outdoor pursuits in the beautiful setting of mountains, lochs and Caledonian pine forest. This is the remains of the Old Wood of Caledon which once covered the whole country, harbouring wolves and bears, but long since was cleared for timber, fuel and farmland. Try your hand at anything from clay pigeon shooting to off-road driving, or more peaceable activities of birding, cycling, fishing and horse trekking. Don't miss the local cheeses and estate venison in the farm shop.

To the south, a good walk lasting about 1.5 hours leads around lovely Loch an Eilean, with its picturesque remains of a 15th-century castle.

Loch Morlich, 7 miles (11.3km) east of Aviemore, is perfect for water-based activities including sailing, windsurfing and canoeing. There is a very popular camping site, and Glenmore Lodge is a training centre for mountaineers.

To the north of Aviemore, at Carrbridge, the Landmark Forest Adventure theme park has displays on local history and wildlife as well as a treetop walk, adventure playgrounds, a maze and water slides.

Visit

SANTA'S HELPERS

This area of ancient forest is associated with rare native creatures such as wildcats, red squirrels, pine martens and capercaillies. Since the 1950s, however, its also been home to a herd of handsome, horned interlopers originating in Sweden: reindeer. Visit them at the Cairngorm Reindeer Centre in Glenmore Forest Park, where they graze on the hillside.

BOAT OF GARTEN

MAP REF NH9419

Boat of Garten is an attractive little Victorian village on the west bank of the River Spey, between Aviemore and Grantown, and gets its name from the ferry that once operated here (replaced by a more convenient bridge in 1898). It is a key stop on the now preserved and restored Strathspey Steam Railway, and its station was once the point where Highland and Great North of Scotland railway companies swapped trains. The railway currently runs from Aviemore all the way to the little country station at Broomhill, which found unlikely fame as 'Glenbogle' station in the TV series,

Monarch of the Glen. The town also has a challenging golf course, which has been described by some in the golf fraternity as a miniature version of Gleneagles.

Two miles (3.2km) to the east lie the still waters of Loch Garten, in the Abernethy Forest, where ospreys have nested since 1959. The RSPB has a hide there, overlooking the distant nesting site, and from where you can watch the activities of the birds in intriguing close up via a video-link. There are walking trails all through the woods around the loch. Abernethy, a National Nature Reserve, is the biggest Scots pine forest remaining in Britain and home to other interesting birds such as crested tits, crossbills and capercaillies.

Just to the north, the resort village of Nethy Bridge is set amid heather clad hills and native woodland, with the ruins of 13th-century Castle Roy close by and visible from the road. The walls stand up to 25 feet (7.6m) high.

Northeast of Boat of Garten, off the A95, lies the pretty little village of Dulnain Bridge. Its chief attraction is the Speyside Heather Visitor and Garden Centre at Skye of Curr, where you can purchase display heathers. There is also a garden centre, an antiques shop, an art gallery, and an interesting restaurant dedicated to the Clootie Dumpling.

Insight

CLOOTIE DUMPLING

The Clootie Dumpling is a suet pudding, or dumpling, traditionally wrapped and boiled in a cloth – the word 'clout' is the broad Scots for a cloth. The puddings are usually sweetened, and contain some raisins and currants, orange peel and spices, and are particularly associated with Hogmanay, or New Year. The dumplings can be served boiled, or the cooled pudding can be sliced and the wedges fried in butter.

BRAEMAR & DEESIDE

MAP REF NO1592

When, in 1852, Queen Victoria and her consort Prince Albert picked an estate between Ballater and Braemar on which to build their holiday home, the entire Dee Valley acquired a cachet which it has never quite lost. Members of the royal family still spend their summer holidays at Balmoral Castle, enjoying country sports in the surrounding hills and forests, and the Braemar Gathering in September is the most famous Highland games of them all, predating Victoria's arrival by some 20 years.

Braemar itself is a bustling place, spread over the banks of the Cluny Burn. Braemar Castle lies to the east, an L-plan tower house, converted to a star-fort and barracks in the mid-18th century to guard an important military road. It has reopened to the public, thanks to community effort.

To the west, a narrow road leads upstream to the Linn of Dee, where the river plunges down between polished rocks into foaming pools. This is part of the 72,598-acre (29,380ha) Mar Lodge Estate, managed by the National Trust for Scotland. There are signposted walks. The road ends near a local beauty spot, the Earl of Mar's Punchbowl, where, it is said, the Earl brewed punch in a natural bowl in the rocks before the Jacobite uprising of 1715. A taxing long-distance walk from here heads into the Lairig Ghru pass to Speyside.

From Braemar the A93 follows the meandering of the river as it flows for 60 miles (96km) to the coast at Aberdeen. Ballater is a small granite-built spa town, once the terminus of a railway branch line. This is celebrated at the Old Royal Station, now an information centre which recalls the days when famous guests would alight here on their way to Balmoral. It also has some interesting little shops and an excellent tea room. To the east lies Glen Tanar, with birch woods at the Muir of Dinnet, and good walking over the Grampian hills to the Glens of Angus.

CAIRNGORMS NATIONAL PARK MAP REF NJ0104

In 2003 the Cairngorms were designated Scotland's second national park, which covers a wide area of upland to the east of, and including, the Spey Valley. Over to the south the boundary continues from Dalwhinnie right across to the Glens of Angus, taking in Glen Esk before turning north to pass east of Ballater and up to Glenlivet. The centre of the national park is made up of the high granite plateaux of the Cairngorm mountains, riven by steep sided glens and deep corries, creating a sub-Arctic environment that is unique in Britain. About half the area of the park has been cleared of trees over the centuries, and is now open heather moorland, managed for grouse shooting. Around the margins, ancient areas of native woodland survive, the original forests have been felled and replanted for their timber many times. The park takes in two great river valleys, the Spey and the Dee, and it is along these that most of its small population of about 14,000 live and work, their numbers swelled in summer by visitors looking for outdoor adventure, and in winter by snow-sports enthusiasts.

There's an extensive network of paths in the glens and forests around the Cairngorms, from starting points such as Nethy Bridge, Rothiemurchus, Aviemore, Glenmore, Grantown-on-Spey, Tomintoul, Ballater, Braemar and glens Tanar, Doll and Feshie. More experience is needed to tackle the heights such as Ben Macdhui (4,295 feet/1,309m), Cairn Gorm (4,085 feet/1,245m) and Cairn Toul (4,242 feet/1,293m). There are plenty of great opportunities for cycling, fishing and golf, and watersports are focused on Loch Insh and Loch Morlich. There are ski centres at Cairngorm, the Lecht and Glenshee, and a funicular railway runs to the summit of Cairngorm for the views (for conservation reasons there is no access beyond the summit station during the summer).

Signs of the earliest settlers may be seen in the hummocks of hill-forts such as Dun da lamh, near Laggan, and the mound of a crannog on Loch Kinnord. Queen Victoria was enchanted by this romantic landscape and built her holiday home, Balmoral Castle, at Braemar in 1853, popularising the region and also beginning a royal connection that still holds strong to this day. One of the oddest memorials associated with her is the crown-shaped monument built over a spring in remote Glen Mark, known as the Queen's Well.

BALMORAL CASTLE

Rothiemurchus Estate

The Rothiemurchus Estate is set right on the edge of the remarkable Cairngorm Mountain massif, the vast mountain plateau that was recently designated the UK's largest national park. The estate lies just outside the resort town of Aviemore, the self-styled 'Adventure Capital of the Highlands'. Rothiemurchus is one of best places in Scotland to enjoy swathes of indigenous Caledonian woodland on a ride that steers through Scots pine, birch and juniper forest on an undulating trail that also scoops around a brace of wood-shrouded lochs. There is a real sense of being somewhere genuinely unspoiled and pristine here, with clear evidence of how the land was formed during the last ice age 10,000 years ago, such as rounded hillocks (known locally as 'drumlins'). Wildlife abounds on the route – look out for everything from red squirrels and crossbills, through to capercaillie and pine marten.

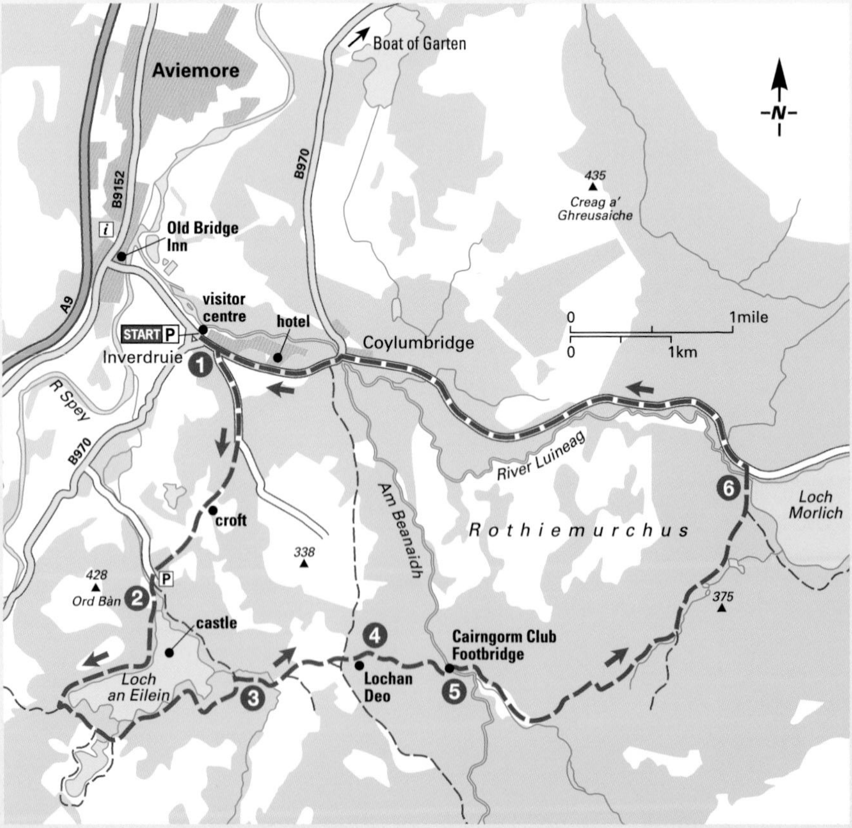

Route Directions

1 From the visitor centre car park head south on a route that quickly takes you into the lush Caledonian forests. En route to the first loch of this cycle ride you pass an old croft (small farm holding).

2 Loch an Eilein, one of Scotland's prettiest lochs, unfurls after you pass the car park (the car route comes in further to the west). The 'Loch of the Island' is named after the small islet that nestles in the middle of the silvery blue water, which is topped off with a picturesque old abandoned castle. Cycle right around or just skirt the northern fringes if you are short on time.

3 Breaking east the trail delves on into a thick forest that is alive with lots of little lochans. One of the most charming is Lochan Deo, which is set just south of the main forest track between the two main lochs. Hop off your bike for five minutes and take a peak at a lochan that is usually deserted.

4 The trail is now deep within the Caledonian forest. Take time to stop and listen to the singing of the birds and for rustles amongst the trees as this is deer country with myriad other wildlife also to be found in the woodland undergrowth.

5 Cross the Cairngorm Club Footbridge, the footbridge which sweeps you over Am Beanaidh. It is a pleasant spot with the water rushing below. The rocky banks make a good place to relax for a moment before pushing on to Loch Morlich.

6 Loch Morlich is a popular place for watersports and has stunning views of the Cairngorm mountains on a clear day. There is a beach on the eastern shores of the loch by the watersports centre. From Loch Morlich turn left and the route breaks back west following the road to Inverdruie, with patches of cycling trail offering an alternative along the way.

Route facts

DISTANCE/TIME 14 miles (22.5km) 3h

MAP OS Explorer 403 Cairn Gorm & Aviemore

START Inverdruie Car Park, grid ref: NH902109

TRACKS Decent tracks and woodland trails, some sections of road

GETTING TO THE START Five-minute drive from Aviemore on the B970 or 15-minute cycle on the same road.

CYCLE HIRE Rothiemurchus Visitor Centre, Inverdruie. Tel: 01479 812345

THE PUB The Old Bridge Inn, 23 Dalfaber Road, Aviemore. Tel: 01479 811137; www.oldbridgeinn.co.uk

A walk to Lochan a' Choire

A fairly challenging linear walk, sometimes over fairly rocky and rugged ground, through regenerating clusters of woodlands leading to the outflow of Lochan a' Choire, a stunning viewpoint for the old crag walls of Coire Ardair.

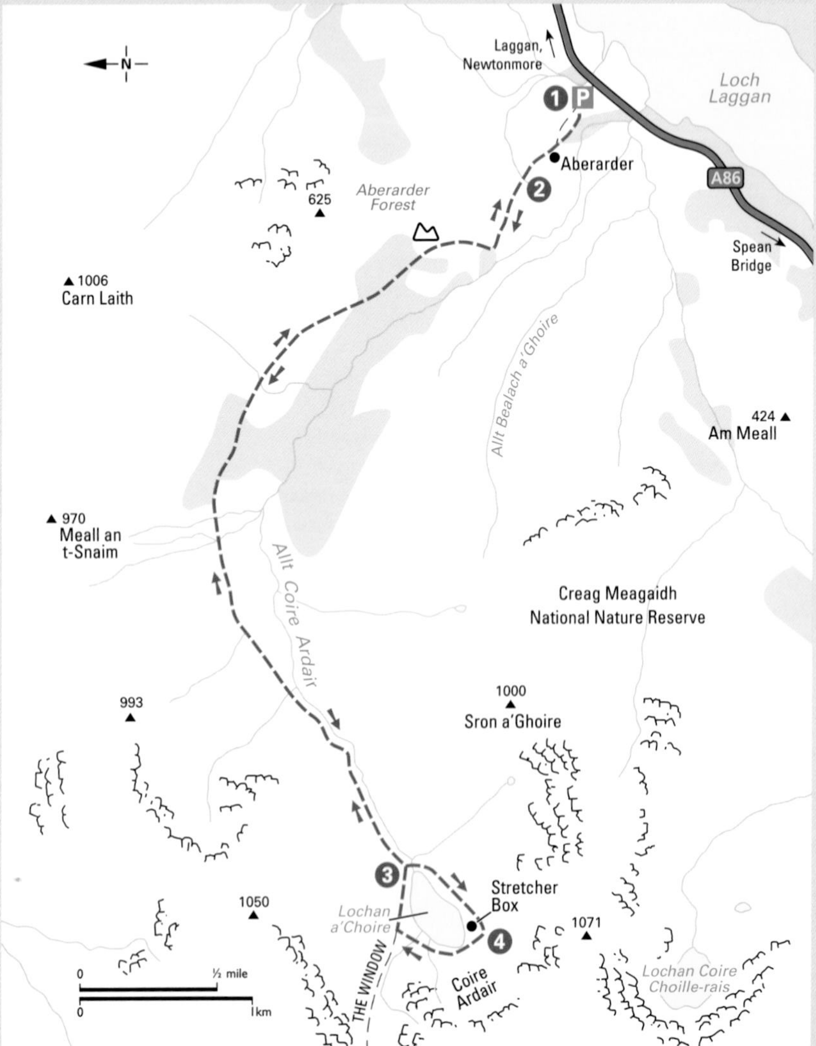

Route Directions

1 A new path runs alongside the grey gravel track, leading to Aberarder farm. Here there's an information area and a bench under a roof. Pass to the right of the buildings following a footprint waymarker on to a rebuilt path.

2 The well-built path rises through bracken, then crosses a boggy area. It heads up the valley of Allt Coire Ardair, keeping a little way up the right-hand side, becoming steeper as it ascends through an area of regenerating birch trees. Now the crags of Coire Ardair come into sight ahead. The path crosses many small streams – here it is still being reconstructed. It bends left, slightly downhill, to join the main river. Tiny rowan trees can be seen attempting to regenerate among the heather. Wild flowers in the boggy ground include the pink or white pyramids of the heath spotted orchid (the leaves have the spots). The path winds gently near the stream, then suddenly to the outflow of Lochan a Choire.

3 The outflow is a fine viewpoint for the crag walls of Coire Ardair. These walls are too loose and overgrown for rock climbing, but when covered in snow and hoarfrost give excellent sport for winter mountaineers. The circuit of the lochan is considerably more rugged than the path up the glen, and could be omitted if the outflow stream is too full, or if a picnic is preferred. Cross the outflow stream near where it emerges from the lochan and follow a trace of path round the shore to the notable clump of boulders marked by a stretcher box. (The stretcher is used for removing mountain casualties from the foot of the crags.) One of the boulders forms a small cave, with a spring running through it. A vigorous rowan tree, seeded where deer can't get at it, shows that without grazing pressure this glen would be wooded even at this altitude of 2,000 feet (610m).

4 After the boulder cave you must cross rocks and scree. This short section is awkward. Once past the head of the lochan, slant up away from the shore. A path descends from high on the left, coming out of the notch called the Window. Join this and turn down to the loch's outflow (Point 3 again). Quite clearly there's no way out of this dead-end valley that doesn't involve serious mountain walking – or one of those winter climbs up the icy gullies. Return down the valley by the outward path.

Route facts

DISTANCE/TIME 8 miles (12.9km) 4h15

MAP OS Explorer 401 Loch Laggan & Creag Meagaidh

START Nature reserve car park at Aberarder track end beside Loch Laggan, grid ref: NN 483872

TRACKS Mostly good, wet and stony in places, there are no stiles

GETTING TO THE START Loch Laggan lies alongside the A86 between Fort William and Kingussie. From Fort William follow the road, passing through Spean Bridge and then tracking the River Spean to the Loch. The nature reserve car park is on your right, just before a turning on the left for Aberarder.

THE PUB Monadhliath Hotel, Lagganbridge, Newtonmore PH20 1BT. Tel: 01528 544276; www.lagganbridge.com

CULLODEN MAP REF NH7246

The Battle of Culloden marked the end of Stuart ambitions to reclaim the throne of Britain from the Hanoverians. On this bleak and desolate moorland east of Inverness, 5,000 Highlanders under the command of the Young Pretender – Bonnie Prince Charlie – faced 9,000 troops led by the Duke of Cumberland. It was 16th April 1746, a day of bitter cold, with snow flurries. The Highlanders, used to short skirmishes, were no match for the disciplined and well-armed soldiers, and despite courageous fighting were swiftly defeated. Cumberland ordered that no prisoners should be taken.

Although it can be very crowded in summer, Culloden remains a moving place. The 1,200 Highlanders who died were buried in clan graves, marked by small, weathered stones. The 76 English dead lie in the Field of the English. Coloured flags fly over the battlefield to mark the disposition of the armies, and the focal point of the area is a large 19th-century memorial cairn, built where the fighting was most ferocious.

The excellent Visitor Centre has clear explanations of the battle, its causes and its aftermath. Prince Charles fled to the hills and eventually escaped to France. The clans were ruthlessly suppressed – the kilt, tartan, the Gaelic language and even the bagpipes were proscribed.

FORRES MAP REF NJ0354

The ancient market town of Forres, on the River Findhorn, was once plagued by witches. William Shakespeare made full use of this in Macbeth (c1606), when he set scenes with the three 'weird sisters' in the area. Three more witches, burned to death, are commemorated with an iron-bound stone in the town. Forres' importance, hinted at in some of its grander buildings, was eclipsed by that of Elgin in the 13th century. Sueno's Stone, on the eastern outskirts, is a Pictish cross-slab which stands 20 feet (6m) tall and is believed to date from the 9th or 10th centuries. The sandstone is intricately carved in five sections with vivid scenes from an unidentified and bloody battle, and is now protected from the elements by a huge glass box. Southeast of the town, Cluny Hill is the highest point, topped by an octagonal tower, raised in 1806 to commemorate Lord Nelson. It is believed to be the first such monument in Britain, and provides a magnificent viewpoint. To the south of Forres, the Dallas Dhu Historic Distillery is preserved by Historic Scotland.

Remarkably, Pluscarden Abbey is the only medieval foundation in Britain still used for its original purpose. To the east of Forres, the monastery is the home of 21 Benedictine monks, and a haven of spiritual retreat for both men and women. The monastery was founded in 1230 by Alexander II, and during the Reformation in the 16th century was gradually abandoned. In 1943 Benedictine monks began its restoration and in 1974 it was granted abbey status. Today the white-habited monks work in the grounds and workshops and care for the abbey buildings. These centre on the massive abbey church, where ancient stonework and frescoes contrast with modern stained glass.

LOCH AN EILEIN

Loch an Eilein's Castle and Ord Ban

A relatively easy walk, around Loch an Eilein and its castle, surrounded by ancient pines and the mountains rising majestically behind. Walk quietly with binoculars and you may see some of the unique birdlife that exists in the forest including the small crested tit and the stout Scottish crossbill. Ospreys used to nest in the castle ruins, and though they are unlikely to return to this popular island, you might see them elsewhere as they strike for a trout.

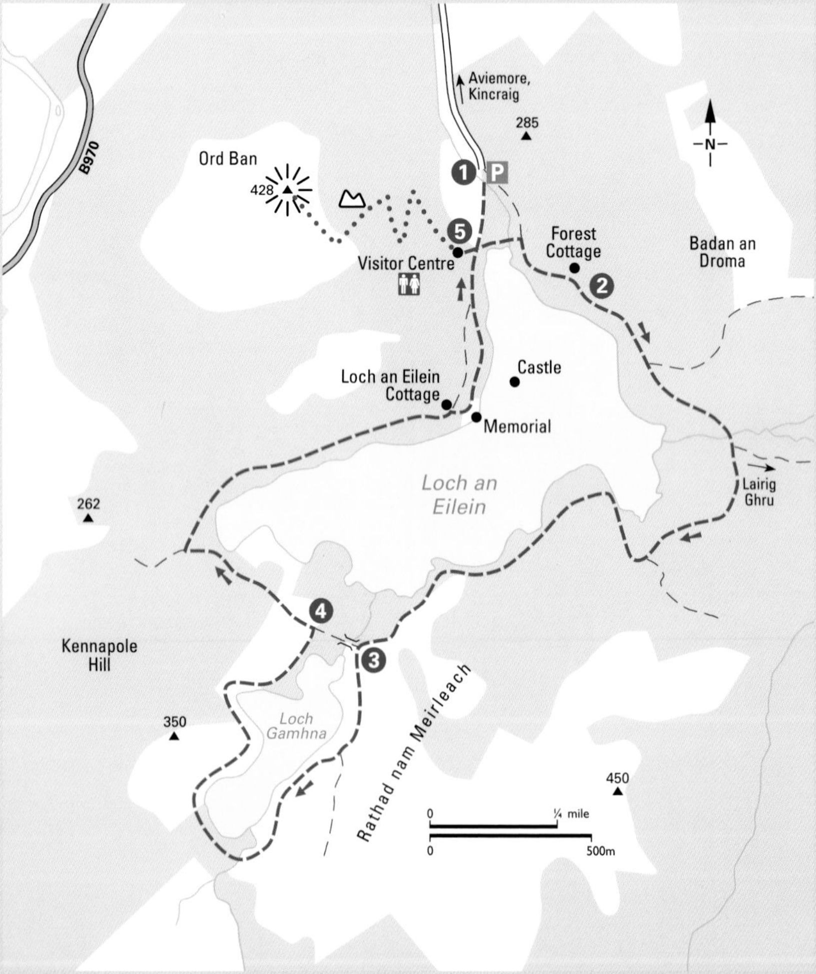

Route Directions

1 From the end of the car park at the beginning of the walk, a made-up path leads to the visitor centre. Turn left to cross the end of Loch an Eilein, then turn right on a smooth sandy track. The loch shore is near by on the right. There are small paths leading down to it if you wish to visit. Just past a red-roofed house, a deer fence runs across, with a gate.

2 The track now becomes a wide, smooth path, which runs close to the loch side. After a bridge, the main track forks right to pass a bench backed by a flat boulder. The smaller path on the left leads high into the hills and through the famous pass of the Lairig Ghru, eventually to Braemar. After crossing a stream at a low concrete footbridge, the path bends right for 120 yards (110m) to a junction. Just beyond you'll find a footbridge with wooden handrails.

3 To shorten the walk, cross this footbridge and continue along the main track, passing Point 4 in another 170 yards (155m). For a longer walk, turn left before the footbridge on to a narrower path that will pass around Loch Gamhna. This second loch soon appears on your right-hand side. Where the path forks, keep right to pass along the loch side, across its head (rather boggy) and back along its further side, to rejoin the wider path around Loch an Eilein. Turn left here.

4 Continue around Loch an Eilein, with the water on your right, to a reedy corner of the loch and a bench. About 55 yards (50m) further, the path turns sharply right, signposted 'footpath'. After a gate, turn right to the loch side and a memorial to Major General Brook Rice who drowned here while skating. Follow the shore to the point opposite the castle, then back up to the wide track above. A deer fence on the left leads back to the visitor centre.

5 From here, a stiff climb (500 feet/152m) can be made on to the rocky little hill of Ord Ban, a superb viewpoint. Cross a ladder stile immediately to the right of the toilet block and follow the deer fence to the right for 150 yards (137m), to a point behind the car park. Just behind one of the lowest birches on the slope, a small indistinct path zig-zags up the steep slope. It slants to the left to avoid crags, then crosses a small rock slab (take care if wet) and continues on to the summit. Descend by the same path.

Route facts

DISTANCE/TIME 4.25 miles (6.8km) 1h45

MAP OS Explorer 403 Cairn Gorm & Aviemore

START Estate car park near Loch an Eilein, grid ref: NH 897084

GETTING TO THE START Loch an Eilein is located approximately 3 miles (4.8km) south of Aviemore, in the Cairngorms National Park. From the town centre take the B9152 south and then turn left onto the B970. Where the road forks turn right to continue southwards and after about half a mile (800m) turn left onto a minor road leading to the loch. The car park is located at the end of the road.

TRACKS Wide smooth paths, optional steep hill with high ladder stile

THE PUB The Old Bridge Inn, Dalfaber Road, Aviemore. Tel: 01479 811137; www.oldbridgeinn.co.uk

KINGUSSIE MAP REF NH7500

The little town of Kingussie lies in the beautiful Spey Valley, once the capital of the ancient area of Badenoch, and with a history that dates back to pre-Pictish times. Today it is best known as home to the Highland Folk Museum, a place with fascinating indoor and outdoor exhibits. In fact, the museum occupies two sites, the other being situated at Newtonmore, to the south. The main house here contains traditional furniture and bygones, and a representation of a Highland kitchen; in the grounds you will find a reconstructed Hebridean mill, a salmon smokehouse in addition to a primitive blackhouse from Lewis. There are regular craft demonstrations and participation during the summer.

Half a mile ((800m) southeast of Kingussie are the impressive Ruthven Barracks, dramatically set on a grassy mound, formerly the site of a castle, and built in 1718 in order to subdue the Highlands, following the 1715 rebellion. Despite being set on fire by the fleeing Jacobite army in 1746, there are still considerable remains. The garrison here guarded General Wade's military road, leading from Glen Truim in the south.

The adjacent Insh Marshes Reserve (RSPB), an important site for breeding waders and wintering waterfowl, has hides and nature trails. There is also a guided tour. You can walk from here to beautiful Glen Tromie.

Just to the north of Kingussie, off the B9152, is the noted Highland Wildlife Park, an extensive reserve and exhibition of themed habitats dedicated to Scottish wildlife, and part of the Royal Zoological Society of Scotland (the owners of Edinburgh Zoo). A driving tour takes in herds of red deer, as well as ancient breeds of bison and horse, before you explore the rest on foot. Look out for otters, owls, boars, Arctic foxes, wildcat and eagles. You can also take a guided tour. The centre is perhaps best known for its collection of wolves, and a raised walkway takes visitors safely into the heart of their (well-fenced) enclosure. The last wild wolf in Scotland was killed in 1743. The centre's newest arrival is a polar bear named Mercedes, originally rescued from Churchill in Canada.

The nearby village of Kincraig is the access point for Loch Insh, popular for watersports, and its ski school has a dry ski slope (200 feet/60m). A church on the loch shore reputedly stands on a site where worship has been continuous since the 6th century.

Kingussie is just 12 miles (20km) from Aviemore ski resort.

SPEYSIDE MAP REF NJ0328

The Spey is one of the foremost salmon rivers in Scotland, flowing northeast from its source on Craig a' Cleat, in the Monadhliath Mountains along a broad strath, or valley, finally reaching the sea at Spey Bay, to the west of Buckie. Although it starts in the mountainous Highlands, its lower reaches are more characteristic of lowland scenery. Along its course, it is fed by streams from high in the Cairngorms, including the Feshie and the Nethy.

The river itself is unnavigable, but the Speyside Way long-distance footpath follows its route for 84 miles (135km) from the police station at Aviemore to the coast, passing Grantown-on-Spey, Cromdale and the Craigellachie Forest, with spur paths joining from Tomintoul and Dufftown.

The Spey Valley is equally renowned for the quality of its malt whisky – you'll not have to travel far without spotting the distinctive pointed chimney-caps of a distillery, for there are more than 30 along the river and its tributaries. Pick up the official 75-mile Malt Whisky Trail for a tour of some of Scotland's finest. Some distilleries that welcome visitors include Glenfiddich, founded by William Grant in 1887 at Dufftown, and the Aberlour Distillery (Walkers Shortbread is also made in Aberlour. There is also a factory shop).

Grantown-on-Spey is one of the largest settlements along the riverbank. The township was planned out in 1765, and has a spacious, genteel feel to it today. Its creator was James Grant, and the arrival of the railway here in 1863 heralded the town's popularity as a health resort. The railway folded in the 1960s, and the town is now better known as a centre for anglers, and walkers keen to explore the Cairngorms. Its story is told in the local museum.

The landscapes and settlements of the upper reaches of the Spey, between Loch Laggan and Grantown-on-Spey, made the perfect backdrop for the popular TV series, *Monarch of the Glen*. Laggan village doubled as 'Glenbogle', and the Victorian mansion of Ardverikie (private) on its shores provided the main setting. Location hunters should check the leaflet *Monarch of the Glen Country*.

Insight

SHINTY

Kingussie is known as a stronghold of the Gaelic sport of shinty. It's a team game similar to hockey, and the highlight of the shinty players' year is the Camanachd Cup Final, held in September in different venues across the country.

Visit

THE COOPER'S CRAFT

None of the distilleries of Strathspey could thrive without the wooden barrels or casks in which the spirit is left to mature. For an insight into the cooper's skill, you can visit the family-run, fully working Speyside Cooperage just south of Craigellachie. Oak for the barrel staves is largely imported from the US, and the cooperage produces around 100,000 casks a year for shipping around the world – oak is preferred for its qualities of 'breathing'.

Visit

EARLY CAIRNS

The fascinating Clava Cairns near Culloden open a window on our remote ancestors. A site of major archaeological importance, and beautifully set among beech trees, it has three large stone burial mounds, each surrounded by a circle of standing stones. They were probably built between about 2000 and 1500 BC. The two outer cairns, still partly covered in small boulders, have stone-lined passages to the centre. The northeast cairn has an interesting series of cup marks on one of the larger boulders. The middle one is hollow, though with no passage. Instead, it has rough cobbled pavements leading away from it. Clava Cairns is part of a whole series of such monuments found only in the region of the Moray Firth.

East of Inverness

Legend and history come to life in this scenic Highland tour which takes you to the east of Inverness. It's a reasonably long distance to drive so you may want to stay overnight en route and take a couple of days to complete the drive. The tour starts at Culloden, a name most people will be familiar with from history lessons on the great battle here. You continue on to two castles, Cawdor and Brodie, and on to the religious community and eco-village at Findhorn.

Route Directions

1 From the Culloden Battlefield & Visitor Centre head west on the B9006 to reach the A9. Join the A9 and follow it to Inverness.
Inverness, 'the Capital of the Highlands' is a working city but also a tourist hub, and, for many, the gateway to Loch Ness .

2 Drive out of Inverness on the A96, travelling through the flatlands south of the Moray Firth. Turn left onto the B9039 to reach the small fishing village of Ardersier, then take the B9006 to Fort George, a distance of 12 miles (19km).
Fort George was constructed between 1748 and 1769 on a narrow spit of land which protrudes out into the Moray Firth, facing Chanonry Point on the Black Isle. With many landward defences, the site originally covered 12 acres (5ha), and was designed to accommodate a garrison of over 2,000 men. The fort, named after George II, was set here to protect Inverness from seaward attack, and as part of the violent backlash to subdue the Highlands after the battle of Culloden. It is unaltered, a superb example of an artillery fort.

3 Return to Ardersier, then follow the B9006 and the B9090 to Cawdor Castle.
This 14th-century castle is associated with the play *Macbeth*. Kilravock Castle (private) stands to the west, the 15th-century family seat of the Roses and in the shadow of its more famous neighbour. It can number both Bonnie Prince Charlie and his nemesis, the Duke of Cumberland, among its visitors in the hours before Culloden (1746).

4 Continue on the B9090 and follow it to Nairn.
Comic actor Charlie Chaplin (1889–1977) liked to take his holidays at this prosperous resort town, with its fine beach, good golf course and activities for all the family. Villas and hotels spread back from old Fishertown by the shore, where the former little fishermen's cottages are so tightly packed together. The harbour dates from 1820, and was designed by engineer Thomas Telford.

5 Leave by the A96, passing Auldearn, site of a major battle between Covenanters and Royalists in 1645. Drive down this road through the shady plantation of Culbin Forest. Turn left for a visit to Brodie Castle.
A Z-plan tower house dating back to 1567, Brodie Castle is set in attractive parkland that is famous for its spring show of daffodils. Remodelled into a comfortable home in the 19th century, it remained in the private hands of the Brodie family until 1980, after which it passed to the National Trust for Scotland. The family's collection of fine art, books and furniture is outstanding, and includes many works from the 17th-

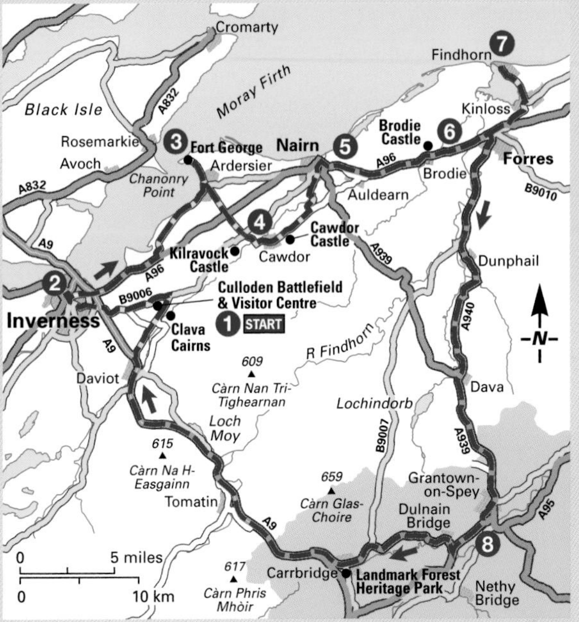

century, from Dutch masters to the Scottish Colourists.

6 Regain the A96, and stay on this road into Forres. Continue on the A96, then turn left at the B9011 and follow this road to Findhorn.

Ever vulnerable from the sea and shifting sand dunes, this is the third village on the site to be called Findhorn – the first village was buried by sand in 1694, the second washed away in 1701. Once a major port, the harbour is now given over to pleasure craft. In 1962 the Findhorn Community was founded here by Peter and Eileen Caddy and Dorothy Maclean to create a more spiritual and sustainable way of living. This thriving community, now has around 300 permanent residents, and supports an extensive holistic education programme and also boasts an eco-village.

7 Return along the B9011 and A96 to Forres. Head south on the A940 and join the A939 for Grantown-on-Spey, a distance of 27 miles (43km).

Grantown-on-Spey lies at the edge of the Speyside whisky country, and makes a useful touring centre. The village was planned in the late 18th century by Sir James Grant, and the arrival of the railway in 1863 heralded its popularity as a health resort. The railway was lost in the 1960s, but the town is still popular with walkers and anglers, and in winter accommodates some of the overspill of skiers from nearby Aviemore.

8 Leave on the A95 towards Aviemore, and at Dulnain Bridge turn on to the A938 to Carrbridge, noted for its picturesque old bridge of 1717, and the Landmark Forest Adventure Park. Continue on the A938 and join the A9, heading towards Inverness. Just after Daviot, turn right on the B851. Turn left at the B9006 and follow it to the major battle site of Culloden Moor where the tour started.

Just east of Culloden, a minor road (B9091) passes Clava Cairns, three of the most important chambered cairns in the country, dating from the Bronze Age (free access). The two outer ones are passage graves, topped with a massive flat slab. The perimeters of all three are marked by a ring of standing stones, often carved with 'cup' marks.

PLACES OF INTEREST

Aberlour Distillery
High Street, Aberlour,
Tel: 01340 881249

Balmoral Castle
Ballater.
Tel: 01339 742534;
www.balmoralcastle.com

Braemar Castle
Braemar.
Tel: 01339 741600

Cairngorm Mountain Railway
Cairngorm Ski Area,
by Aviemore.
Tel: 01479 861261; www.
cairngormmountain.co.uk

Corgarff Castle (HS)
Strathdon.
Tel: 01975 651460

Culloden Battlefield Visitor Centre (NTS)
Culloden Moor, Inverness.
Tel: 0844 493 2159

Dallas Dhu Historic Distillery
Mannachie Road, Forres.
Tel: 01309 676548

Dalwhinnie Distillery
Dalwhinnie.
Tel: 01540 672219

Elgin Cathedral
King Street, Elgin.
Tel: 01343 547171

Findhorn Community
The Park, Findhorn
Tel: 01309 690311;
www.findhorn.org

Glenfiddich Distillery
Dufftown.
Tel: 01340 820373;
www.glenfiddich.com

Glenlivet Distillery
Ballindalloch.
Tel: 01340 821720; www.
maltwhiskydistilleries.com

Grantown Museum
Burnfield Avenue,
Grantown-on-Spey.
Tel: 01479 872478;
www.grantownmuseum.co.uk

Highland Folk Museum
Duke Street, Kingussie.
Tel: 01540 673551;
www.highlandfolk.com

Loch Garten Osprey Centre
Abernethy.
Tel: 01479 831476;
www.rspb.org.uk

Mar Lodge Estate (NTS)
Braemar.
Tel: 0844 493 2172;
www.marlodgeestate.org.uk

Moray Firth Wildlife Centre
Tugnet, Spey Bay.
Tel: 01343 820339;
www.wdcs.org

Old Royal Station
Station Square, Ballater.
Tel: 01339 755306

Pluscarden Abbey
Pluscarden, Elgin.
www.pluscardenabbey.org

Royal Lochnagar Distillery
Crathie, Ballater.
Tel: 01339 742700;
www.discoveringdistilleries.
com

Speyside Cooperage
Dufftown Road,
Craigellachie.
Tel: 01340 871108; www.
speysidecooperage.co.uk

Speyside Heather Visitor and Garden Centre
Skye of Curr, Dulnain Bridge.
Tel: 01479 851359;
www.heathercentre.com

Strathspey Steam Railway
Aviemore, Boat of Garten.
Tel: 01479 810725;
www.strathspeyrailway.net

FOR CHILDREN

Cairngorm Reindeer Centre
Reindeer House, Glenmore.
Tel: 01479 861228; www.
cairngormreindeer.co.uk

Highland Wildlife Park
Kincraig, by Kingussie.
Tel: 01540 651270;
www.highlandwildlifepark.org

Landmark Forest Adventure Park
Carrbridge.
Tel: 01479 841613;
www.landmarkpark.co.uk

SHOPPING

A'Anside Studios
5 Main Street, Tomintoul.
Tel: 01479 872074;
Scottish arts and crafts.

Baxters Highland Village
Fochabers, on the A96.
Tel: 01343 820666;
www.baxters.com
Shops at the soup factory.

Ellis Brigham
9–10 Grampian Road,
Aviemore.
Tel: 01479 810175;
www.ellis-brigham.com
Outdoor sports gear.

Johnston's of Elgin Cashmere Visitor Centre
Newmill, Elgin.
Tel: 01343 554099; www.johnstonscashmere.com

SPORTS & ACTIVITIES

ADVENTURE SPORTS

Full On Adventure
24 Cairngorm Avenue, Aviemore.
Tel: 07885 835838; www.fullonadventure.co.uk

Active Outdoor Pursuits
Grampian Road, Aviemore.
Tel: 01479 780000; www.activeoutdoorpursuits.com

Glenmore Lodge
By Aviemore.
Tel: 01479 861256; www.glenmorelodge.org.uk

Rothiemurchus Estate
By Aviemore.
Tel: 01479 812345; www.rothiemurchus.net

CYCLING

Cycle Highlands
The Pavilion, Victoria Road, Ballater.
Tel: 013397 55864; www.cyclehighlands.com

FISHING

Fishdee
Fish Pal Ltd.
Tel: 01573 470612; www.fishdee.co.uk

Glen Tanar Estate
Brooks House, Glen Tanar, Aboyne.
Tel: 013398 86451; www.glentanar.co.uk

GOLF

Abernethy Golf Club
Nethybridge.
Tel: 01479 821305; www.abernethygolfclub.com
9 holes.

Grantown-on-Spey Golf Club
Golf Course Road.
Tel: 01479 872079; www.grantownonspeygc.co.uk
18 holes.

Kingussie Golf Club
Gynack Road, Kingussie.
Tel: 01540 661600; www.kingussie-golf.co.uk
18 holes.

HORSE-RIDING

Glen Tanar Equestrian Centre
Glen Tanar, Aboyne.
Tel: 013398 86448

Tomintoul Riding Centre
St Bridget Farm, Tomintoul.
Tel: 01807 580210; www.highlandhooves.co.uk

LONG-DISTANCE PATH

Speyside Way
Aviemore to Buckie, 65 miles (105km)
www.speysideway.org

WATERSPORTS

Loch Insh Watersports Outdoor Activiy Centre
Kincraig. Tel: 01540 651272; www.lochinsh.com

Loch Morlich Watersports Centre
Glenmore Forest Park, by Aviemore.
Tel: 01479 861221; www.lochmorlich.com

WILDLIFE TOURS

Speyside Wildlife
Aviemore.
Tel: 01479 812498; www.speysidewildlife.co.uk

WINTER SPORTS

Aviemore Ski & Snowboard Hire
Unit 4, Myrtlefield Shopping Centre. Tel: 01479 811711; www.osa-travel.co.uk

Glenshee Ski Centre
Cairnwell, by Braemar.
Tel: 013397 41320; www.ski-glenshee.co.uk

Lecht 2090 Ski and Multi-Activity Centre
Strathdon, on A939.
Tel: 01975 651440; www.lecht.co.uk

EVENTS & CUSTOMS

Abernethy
Highland Games, Aug

Braemar
Braemar Gathering, early Sep

Carrbridge
World Porridge Making Championships, early Oct

Grantown-on-Spey
Highland Games, Aug

Speyside
Sprit of Speyside Whisky Festival, end Apr–May

LOCH AN UVIE

Tea Rooms

Brodie Countryfare

Brodie, by Forres, Morayshire IV36 2TD
Tel: 01309 641555; www.brodiecountryfare.com

On the A96 close to Brodie Castle, this busy shopping complex offers a foodhall and good delicatessen full of rich aromas. Only the best local ingredients are served up in the restaurant, whether it's freshly baked scones with your cup of tea or a more substantial meal.

The Clootie Dumpling

Speyside Heather Visitor & Garden Centre, Skye of Curr, Dulnain Bridge, Highland PH26 3PA.
Tel: 01479 851359; www.heathercentre.com

Tea, coffee, sandwiches, speciality soups and other traditional home-made foods are available all day – but the highlight has got to be the Clootie Dumpling, which is served in 21 different ways.

Culloden Visitor Centre

Culloden Moor, Inverness, Highland, IV2 5EU
Tel: 0844 493 2159

The lovely café/restaurant in the new visitor centre here serves light lunches and snacks, including vegetable soups complimented by freshly baked cheese scones.

Gordon's Tearoom

20 Mar Road, Braemar AB35 5YL
Tel: 013397 41247

This friendly corner tea room in the middle of Braemar village serves tea and coffee with home-baked cakes and scones, as well as snacks, hearty home-made soups and more substantial meals from the blackboard menu.

Pubs

Cawdor Tavern

The Lane, Cawdor, Highland IV12 5PX
Tel: 01667 404777

Close to the famous castle, this pub is in a former estate building. The pub has an excellent reputation for its food, offering main courses such as prime beef, steak pie and haggis. There are good children's facilities, and dogs are allowed. Beers include Raven Ale.

Lairhillock Inn

Netherley, near Stonehaven AB39 3QS
Tel: 01569 730001
www.lairhillock.co.uk

A former coaching inn, this lovely old country pub offers real ale in the bar and fresh local and regional produce on the menu, including Aberdeen Angus beef. The Lairhillock lasagne is a lunchtime treat, layering minced venison, pork and beef and topped with a wild mushroom sauce. More formal dining is available in the Crynoch restaurant.

The Old Bridge Inn

Dalfaber Road, Aviemore, Highland PH22 1PU
Tel: 01479 810270

A cosy, friendly Highland pub overlooking the River Spey, with an attractive riverside garden as a bonus for high summer. Bar meals include lamb chops with redcurrant jelly, Aberdeen Angus steaks, or perhaps chicken breast marinated in lime, yoghurt and coriander. There's also a large selection of malt whiskies to sample.

Tipsy Laird

68 High Street, Kingussie, Highland PH21 1HZ
Tel: 01540 661334

Look out for venison burgers, freshly prepared soup, and toasted ciabattas on the light lunch menu at this popular walkers' and outdoor enthusiasts' pub in Kingussie. Simple, hostel-style accommodation is also available here.

URQUHART CASTLE

Skye & Northern Highlands

Northern Scotland contains some of the country's most dramatic features, from the slash of the Great Glen and mystical Loch Ness, Britain's deepest freshwater lake, to Ben Nevis, its highest mountain. As the landscapes are bigger and the climate harsher, so the population is sparser. Exceptions are found on the west coast, where a fabulous garden flourishes in the comparative warmth at Inverewe. Wildlife watching is a key attraction, with otters, dolphins, seals, and occasionally whales.

CALEDONIAN CANAL

PORTREE

FIRTH OF DORNOCH

Unmissable attractions

Ride to the top of the Nevis range for stunning views of the craggy mountains and deep lochs below...visit the Museum and Art Gallery at Inverness where you can learn about the geological and historical make-up of the area...wander through the impressive gardens established at Inverewe by Osgood MacKenzie...marvel at the engineering mastery of the Caledonian Canal and its complex series of lochs...climb aboard the Western Line railway, one of the most scenic journeys in Britain...stand on the shore of Loch Ness and summon the legendary monster to appear...join a whale-watching cruise off the coast from Fort William or scan the ocean for friendly bottlenose dolphins...explore the dramatic landscape on the romantic Isle of Skye.

1

2

3

4

1 **Glenfinnan Valley**
The *Jacobite* steam train puffs gently through the Glenfinnan Valley where it stops at Mallaig.

2 **Inverewe Garden**
Osgood Mackenzie's vision in the 19th century resulted in these stunning gardens on a steep rocky promontory near Loch Ewe.

3 **Isle of Skye**
Pony-trekking is a leisurely way to see Skye.

4 **Rum**
The view towards Rum, a National Nature Reserve and home to Kinloch Castle.

5 **Caledonian Canal**
Boats moored at Fort Augustus on the canal.

6 **Inverness Castle**
This 19th-century castle was built on the site of an 11th-century castle which was destroyed in 1746.

5

6

APPLECROSS

MAP REF NG7144

Looking north from the picture-postcard village of Plockton, the rugged hills of Applecross fill both the view and the imagination. Until the last century this peninsula was almost as isolated as Knoydart. Rough tracks linked the old settlements along the coast down to Toscaig, and access up from the south was via the breathtakingly spectacular Bealach-na-Ba pass, which rises to some 2,050 feet (624.8m). In 1965 a road was started around the northern margin from Shieldaig, making it a pleasant circular driving route around this remote and beautiful place.

An Irish saint established a religious community here in the 7th century, but it was destroyed in a Viking raid. Today it is hard to believe that 3,000 people once thrived with their cattle in the green, fertile valley around the quiet village of Applecross itself – cleared from the land when the Mackenzies sold it off for a sporting estate; only the outlines of their deserted cottages remain.

Visit

EILEAN DONAN CASTLE

One of the most photographed and romantic castles in Scotland, Eilean Donan is perched on a rock just offshore in Loch Duich, linked to the mainland and a modern visitor centre by a stone bridge. There's been a fortification here since the 13th century and its 14-foot (4.26m) thick walls have withstood the onslaught of both men and the elements. The castle owes its appearance today to restoration between 1912 and 1932, by Lt Col John MacRae-Gilstrap, who had a vision in a dream of how it should look.

Applecross Bay is a welcoming curve of pinkish sand, with an excellent little inn noted for its fresh seafood.

BLACK ISLE MAP REF NH7967

The Black Isle is the fertile spit of land between the Cromarty and Moray firths. The central forested ridge carries the peninsula's older name of Ardmeanach, and was part of lands gifted by Mary, Queen of Scots to her husband (and cousin), Lord Darnley.

Cromarty, set on the northeastern tip of the peninsula, is a delightfully built 18th-century town, an important centre of fishing and commerce until the 19th century, when it was bypassed by the railways. The whitewashed Courthouse Museum tells the town's story, with the aid of computer-controlled, animated figures. Hugh Miller, a 19th-century geologist, social commentator and writer, lived in the little thatched cottage next door. The cottage is now in the care of the National Trust for Scotland. The fossil beach where he worked is 2 miles (3.2 km) away at Eathie.

Fortrose looks out across the Moray Firth. The cathedral was completed in the 15th century, but was then unroofed in the 16th, before Cromwell plundered its great sandstone blocks to build the fortifications in Inverness. On the other side of the spit (once a popular spot for witch-burning but now dedicated to golf) lies Rosemarkie, notable for the magnificent Pictish carvings displayed at the Groam House Museum.

The mudflats of the Beauly Firth attract a large number of birds – over-wintering greylag and pink-footed geese graze the fields around, and a variety of sea ducks, including goldeneye and scoter, may be spotted near the Kessock Bridge.

In the graveyard of the parish church of Avoch, near Rosemarkie, lie the remains of the great Scottish explorer Sir Alexander Mackenzie (1755–1820). Mackenzie travelled to Canada in 1779 and was soon trading furs for the North West Company. Based at Fort Chipewyan on Lake Athabasca, he set out with a team of native Canadian Indians in 1789 to discover a route across the continent, but found instead a long river, which would be named after him, leading up to the Arctic Ocean. In 1793 he became the first white man to cross the Rockies and reach the Pacific.

Activity

DOLPHIN WATCH

Bottlenose dolphins found around the Scottish mainland are some of the largest in the world, and in the Moray Firth area there is currently one of only two resident populations in Britain, with at least 88 individuals identified. Cromarty has become the best place in Britain to see bottlenose dolphins in the wild – boat trips run by Dolphin Ecosse are available throughout the year. There are also whale-watching trips in August and September.

CANNICH MAP REF NH3331

The broad Strath Glass from the north leads to the modern village of Cannich where four valleys meet. Eastwards, down Glen Urquhart, is the prehistoric Corrimony Cairn, still with its stone roof and eleven standing stones. Dramatic Glen Cannich is entered by a winding road between bare mountain tops, with groves of birch and alder. It widens towards Loch Mullardoch and its dam, 9 miles (14.5km) west of Cannich, at 2,385 feet (726.5m), is the longest in Scotland.

The approach to Glen Affric, perhaps the most beautiful of Scottish valleys, passes the popular Dog Falls. Along this 6-mile (9.7km) stretch of Loch Beinn a'Mheadhoin are parking spots, many with fine walks starting from them. On the opposite side is one of the largest remnants of the ancient Caledonian Pine Forest, fenced to keep out deer and allow regeneration. Beyond the loch the road ends, but you can walk on to Loch Affric – a magical scene of clustered hills, birch and pine forest; during the autumn there is dazzling colour and a hint of snow on the peaks. You can also follow the old track up through the mountains to Sheil Bridge in Kintail.

FORT WILLIAM

MAP REF NN1074

Fort William's greatest asset is its close proximity to Ben Nevis, Britain's highest mountain, which stands sentinel over the Nevis range about 7 miles (11.3km) to the north. The town is also at the southern entrance to the Great Glen and at the head of Loch Linnhe, with routes to Badenoch and Skye. But this is not just a place to venture from – it has its own delights too. The idiosyncratic West Highland Museum, famous for the Jacobite collections held there, lives up to its description as 'an old-fashioned museum – it is full of information and

Insight

ATTAINING THE HEIGHTS

Until well into the 19th century everyone thought that soaring Ben Macdhui in the Cairngorms, and not Ben Nevis, was Britain's highest mountain. It was the peak everyone climbed, including Gladstone and even Queen Victoria. She wrote in her journal, 'Nothing could be grander or wilder; the rocks are so grand and precipitous, and the snow on Ben Macdhui has such fine effect.' Like Everest, only recognised as the world's highest mountain in the 19th century, Ben Nevis remained unrecognised until accurate measurement was made by the Ordnance Survey in 1846 and the issue was resolved – Ben Nevis is the highest at 4,406 feet (1,343m), and Ben Macdhui is runner-up at 4,296 feet (1,309m).

surprises' with an eclectic range of displays, including natural history, Highland clothing and crofting. Treasures of the Earth, at Corpach to the west of town, is a huge collection of rare gemstones, crystals and fossils, including Europe's largest uncut emerald. Visitors can also discover how amethyst crystals take a quarter of a million years to grow just 1 inch (2.5cm).

Until recently the tops of Scotland's mountain ranges were the exclusive preserve of the athletic, but now everyone can experience breathtaking views without so much as getting out of breath. Panoramic vistas to the upper slopes of Aonach Mor (4,000 feet/1,219m) open up from enclosed gondola cable cars which cover about 1.5 miles (2.4km) in their climb to an altitude of 2,150 feet (655m). The ascent takes about 15 minutes and at the top, in addition to the views across Loch Lochy, the Great Glen, Loch Eil and the Inner Hebrides, you will find a restaurant, a sports shop, telescopes, interpretative plaques and slide presentations. There are a number of walks but do keep to the paths, both for your own safety and for conservation. Two recommended walks are to Sgurr Finnisg-aig (taking about 20 minutes each way) and to Meal Beag (taking about 30 minutes in each direction).

GAIRLOCH MAP REF NG8076

This popular holiday village with its excellent Heritage Museum is spread around a sunny, sandy bay, with the heights of the delightfully named Flowerdale looming behind. There are superb views out to the islands, and Gairloch lies at the heart of a fine scenic area which takes in the incomparable Loch Maree. West from the village, the road winds around the bay and eventually turns into a track, leading to the former lighthouse at Rubha Reidh. To the south of the bay there are intriguing woody inlets, perfect for exploring in a small boat. Beyond sheltered Badachro the road passes sandy bays to end at Redpoint, but energetic walkers can take the long path to Diabaig on Loch Torridon.

Behind Gairloch the A832 leads to the long stretch of water that is Loch Maree, famous for its fishing. It is surrounded by high mountains and scattered with darkly wooded islands. The highest peak on the northern shore is Slioch (3,219 feet/981m), while to the south Beinn Eighe, with its cap of white quartzite, lies at the heart of Britain's first National Nature Reserve. You can find out about nature trails and picnic spots at the visitor centre at Aultroy, towards the eastern end of the loch.

Isle Maree, by Letterewe, was the site of a 7th-century hermitage, and may even have had much older, druidical connections. Queen Victoria fell in love with the whole area when she visited in 1877, giving her name to the waterfall near Talladale.

GLENELG MAP REF NG8119

The old military road that leads up to Glenelg rockets off the main Kyle of Lochalsh road, climbing rapidly up the Mam Ratagain pass to a fine viewpoint offering stunning views of the lovely Five Sisters of Kintail above Loch Duich. There follows a gentler descent into Glen More, where a side road goes to the six-car turntable ferry that is a romantic summer alternative to the modern bridge to Skye.

The Glenelg road passes the gaunt remains of Bernera Barracks, built in 1722 for Hanoverian troops (ruins fenced off for safety reasons). Continue for 2.5 miles (4km) into Glen Beag for Glenelg's most famous sight – its two brochs. The circular walls of Dun Telve still stand to 33 feet (10m), and are 13 feet (4m) wide at the base. Dun Troddan is more ruined, but in both you can still see the remains of the internal galleries and stairways (open access).

Admirers of Gavin Maxwell's *Ring of Bright Water* will want to go even further along the coast to Sandaig, where the author lived and where he kept his famous otters in the 1950s. The house he called Camusfearna in his books stood near the shore of the bay, but was burned down and then demolished, at his request on his death. Maxwell's ashes lie under a boulder here, and a cairn has an inscription to Edal the otter.

Visit

THE PARALLEL ROADS

In a quiet valley 18 miles (29km) to the northeast of Fort William is a geological phenomenon that is unique in Britain. Glen Roy and its side valleys are marked by three strange parallel lines known as the 'Parallel Roads', not roads at all, but the shorelines of an ancient glacial loch. Towards the end of the last Ice Age, 10,000 years ago, the valley was dammed with ice that melted in three stages, leaving these horizontal ridges along the valley slopes. Scottish Natural Heritage explains it all on an interpretative board above the car park. To get to Glen Roy from Fort William, go north on the A82, turn right on to the A86 at Spean Bridge, then left on an unclassified road at Roy Bridge.

Insight

SCOTS BROCHS

Only Scotland has brochs, those distinct, cooling-tower-shaped structures, built in the Iron Age, from around 500 BC to AD 100. Some 500 sites have been identified, mostly near the sea and in areas where timber was scarce but stone was plentiful. No one knows their function, but they were probably defensive – the name is from Old Norse borg, meaning a fortress. The open interiors had galleries and parapets, and elaborate internal staircases, all carefully constructed. The best-preserved is on Mousa in Shetland.

To Flowerdale Falls

On most summer days, either the harbour porpoise or common dolphin – or possibly both – can be seen, given a little patience, in Loch Gairloch. A loch cruise is the best way to see these creatures. After walking along the Gairloch shoreline, take the fairly easy route up a rocky valley to Flowerdale Waterfall.

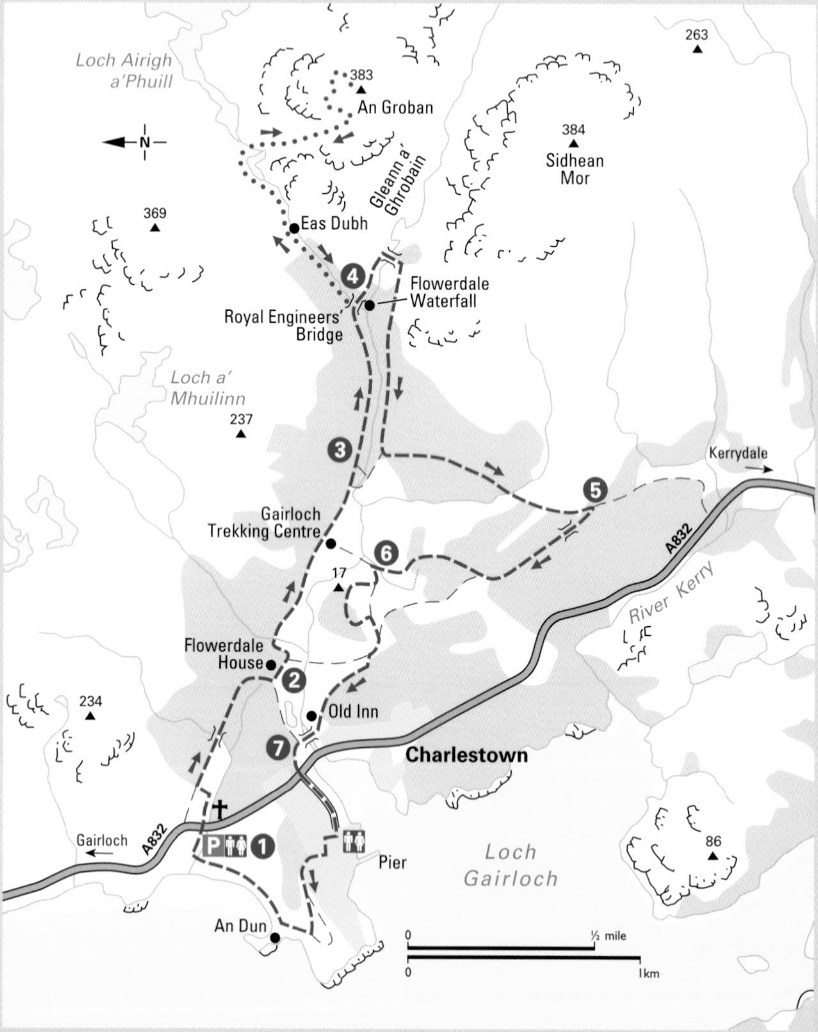

Route Directions

1 Cross the road and head up to the right of the newer cemetery. Turn left at its corner, going into trees to a path above. Turn right until a footbridge leads on to a wide path that soon runs downhill. The main path bends right (green-top waymarker) and down to a tarred driveway.

2 Turn left along a tarred track to pass Flowerdale House.The track passes to the left of a lovely old barn and turns right at a sign for the waterfall to pass Gairloch Trekking Centre. In about 0.25 mile (400m) you pass a timber-surfaced bridge on the right.

3 Follow the main path ahead, still to the left of the stream, to reach a footbridge built by the Royal Engineers, just before you get to Flowerdale Waterfall. (At this point you can divert left on a rough path for an ascent of An Groban. Note that the going can be surprisingly hard.)

4 The main route leads up past the waterfall to cross a footbridge above. It runs up into a wind-blown pine clump, then turns back down the valley. After another footbridge it joins a rough track. You pass a memorial to the blind piper of Gairloch, just before a forest road beside Point 3. Turn left, away from the timber-surfaced bridge, through felled forest that's regenerating naturally (with birch, alder, pine, willow and rowan).

5 A blue-topped pole marks a path to the right with a footbridge. It leads through scrub birch and bracken with blue waymarker poles. The path bends right at an old fence cornerpost and goes down through bracken and birch to pass above and to the left of an enclosed field. Turn right underneath two large oak trees and cross a small stream to an earth track.

6 Turn left for a few steps, until a small bracken path runs up to the right past a waymarked power pole. The path bends left under oaks, then drops to rejoin the earth track. This soon meets a larger track, which is the old road from Loch Maree to Gairloch. Turn right along this, through a couple of gates, to reach the Old Inn at Charlestown.

7 Cross the old bridge, and the main road, towards the pier. Turn right at the signpost for the beach, to a stepped path to the left of Gairloch Chandlery. The tarred path passes to the left of a pinewood, then turns right into the trees. It bends left and emerges to run along the spine of a small headland. Just before being carried out to sea it turns sharp right, and crosses above a rocky bay to the fort (An Dun). A duckboard path runs along the back of the beach, then turns right to the car park.

Route facts

DISTANCE/TIME 5.25 miles (8.4km) 2h45

MAPS OS Explorer 433 Torridon – Beinn Eighe & Liathach or 434 Gairloch & Loch Ewe

START Beach car park, southern end of Gairloch, grid ref: NG 807756 on OS Explorer 433

TRACKS Tracks and smooth paths, mostly waymarked, no stiles

GETTING TO THE START Loch Gairloch forms part of the coast of the North West Highlands. The beach lies on the shore between Charlestown and Gairloch. Follow the A832 north and the car park is located on the left hand side of the road just after exiting Charlestown.

THE PUB The Old Inn, Gairloch. Tel: 0800 542 5444; www.theoldinn.net

Insight

GEOLOGICAL WONDER

The northwest corner of Scotland is largely made up of Lewisian gneiss, around 3,000 million years old and the oldest rock in Britain. Its eastern boundary is marked by the Moine Thrust zone – an erratic line of basal quartzite and pipe rock. Around 780 square miles (2,000sq km) of mountain, peat bog, forest and coastline in this North West Highlands area is now celebrated with the European designation of Scotland's first geopark. Highlights include the mountains of Suilven and Stac Pollaigh, Inchnadamph National Nature Reserve and the sheer cliffs at Cape Wrath.

Insight

CONCRETE BOB'S VIADUCT

The West Highland Railway gives wonderful views down Loch Shiel from the Glenfinnan Viaduct, and the viaduct itself is impressive. It was built when the line from Glasgow, which had struggled across Rannoch Moor to Fort William by 1894, was extended to Mallaig in 1902. Curving over 1,000 feet (308m) over the River Finnan, its 21 concrete arches are up to 100 feet (30.5m) high. The viaduct was designed for Robert MacAlpine (later Sir Robert, founder of the civil engineering firm) whose nickname was Concrete Bob. It is said that buried within the Glenfinnan Viaduct are a horse and cart that fell headlong into the concrete before it set.

Insight

FLOWER POTS TO POT SHOTS

Osgood Mackenzie, creator of Inverewe Garden, was a typical Victorian gentlemen when it came to sport. He was a keen shot and proud of his success. In 1856 alone he records bagging 184 hares, 110 golden plover, 91 rock pigeons, 35 wild duck, 53 snipe and 49 partridges, as well as 1,313 grouse – and this does not include roe deer, ptarmigan, teal and geese.

GLENFINNAN MAP REF NM9080

Glenfinnan will always have a special place in Scottish history, for it was here that the event which Winston Churchill called 'one of the most audacious and irresponsible enterprises in British history' began – the 1745 Jacobite Rising. The monument tower of 1815, with its 1834 figure of a Highlander, may not be on the exact spot where Bonnie Prince Charlie unfurled his father's white and red silk banner, yet it is most romantically set at the head of Loch Shiel, overlooking the wooded Eilean Glean Fhianin and the mountains of Sunart and Moidart. Climb the tower for the best views of the loch.

The clan chiefs were dismayed that the Prince had brought only seven followers, not the French troops they had expected. They were persuaded to join him only by the example of Cameron of Lochiel, who brought 700 men to Glenfinnan for the Prince. So on 19 August 1745 the banner was set flying, the Old Pretender was proclaimed King James III & VIII, with the Prince as his Regent, and the army – still only 1,200 strong – began its campaign. Capturing Edinburgh easily and defeating General Cope in the 15-minute battle at Prestonpans on 21 September, they set out for London. But with little English support and no hope of French help, they turned back at Derby that December and met their doom at Culloden the following April.

The story is vividly told in the Visitor Centre near by, which also traces the Prince's journeys through the Western Highlands and Islands after Culloden.

INVEREWE MAP REF NG8683

Surrounded by barren peat bogs, rocks and water, Inverewe is one of Britain's most remarkable gardens and a must-see for plant-lovers from all over the world. Lying on the same line of latitude as Moscow and Hudson's Bay, the site must have seemed a daunting challenge when Osgood MacKenzie inherited the Inverewe Estate in 1862. Osgood possessed every skill and quality necessary in order to create this wonderful oasis – imagination, vision, perseverance and patience.

First he planted a shelter belt of pines and firs, carted out the rocks and replaced them with hundreds of tonnes of garden soil. Once protected against strong winds, Inverewe could benefit from the warming effects of the North Atlantic Drift. Rhododendrons were planted in profusion, and still provide one of the most spectacular attractions in the early summer. Paths meander between the blooms and beneath the pines, and pass an almost bewildering array of rare and exotic plants, collected from all over the world. Rock gardens are bright with alpines, including many species from New Zealand, and the area named 'Japan' is planted with a variety of tree ferns and palms.

There are wonderful views along the loch from the tip of the garden at Cuddy Rock, and also from the front of the house, built in 1937 after fire destroyed Osgood's original building. Mackenzie died in 1922, and his daughter Mairi, who had maintained and developed his vision, presented the garden to the National Trust for Scotland in 1952.

INVERNESS MAP REF NH6645

Inverness is known as the 'Capital of the Highlands', Scotland's newest city (designated in 2000) and a popular holiday centre, set on the banks of the River Ness at the eastern extremity of the Great Glen. Commanding the east–west facing corridor to Moray and Aberdeen as well as the main north–south route through Scotland, its location has given the town a strategic importance that has resulted in a much chequered history. Inverness was probably well established by the time of St Columba's visit in AD 565. Certainly King Duncan (c1010–1040), notably of Shakespeare's *Macbeth*, had his castle in the town, and various clan chiefs and disaffected Jacobites have stormed through the town over the centuries.

Today Inverness is a busy administrative centre for the Highlands and Islands and presents a mostly 19th-century face. Even the dominating red sandstone walls of Inverness Castle were rebuilt during Victoria's reign as a Sheriff Court and jail, with a monument to Flora Macdonald on the castle esplanade. On the opposite side of the river loom the two massive towers of St Andrew's Episcopal Cathedral, which contains an interesting collection of Russian icons. The refurbished Inverness Museum and Art Gallery has fine examples of Highland artefacts and displays on the archaeology, social and natural history of the Highlands. The museum hosts various exhibitions, performances and talks.

From the museum you can see Craig Phadrig, a vitrified Iron Age fort on a wooded hill west of the River Ness, reached by a steep forest trail from Leachkin Brae. In Huntly Street next to the river you can visit the largest kilt-making workshop in Scotland – Highland House of Fraser's Scottish Kiltmaker.

Visit

THE CURSE OF CALDA HOUSE

Near to the old ruins of the MacLeods' 15th-century Ardvreck Castle you can see the remains of a grand mansion. This was Edderchalder, or Calda House, which was built around 1720 by the up-and-coming Mackenzies. Legend says that the woman who lived there was a witch who had cursed the district in a fit of rage, so that crops failed. Around 1737, after another miserable harvest, the curse was lifted when the house was struck by lightning.

Visit

THE CALEDONIAN CANAL

One of the greatest feats of 19th-century engineering, the 60 mile-long (96km) Caledonian Canal was constructed along the Great Glen by Thomas Telford, who took advantage of the lochs – Lochy, Oich and Ness – which account for about two-thirds of the route. The linking sections of canal have a total of 28 locks, including the famous 'Neptune's Staircase', a series of eight locks at Banavie. Begun in 1803 and finally opened in 1822, the canal was originally constructed to provide a safe route for maritime traffic, which previously had to brave the hazardous seas around the north of Scotland, but the scenic route was soon appreciated by tourists too. By 1900 they were filling three steamboats a day, bound from Inverness to Fort Augustus, Fort William and Oban. Cruise ships still operate on the canal, and there is a visitor centre at Fort Augustus.

INVERPOLLY MAP REF NC1412

North of Ullapool the habitation is sparse and the landscape becomes altogether bigger and wilder, with giant, bare mountains looming out of bleak, bitter moorland.

The Inverpolly National Nature Reserve, managed by Scottish Natural Heritage, offers access to this fine, dramatic countryside in all its glory, and the visitor centre at Knockan is a good place to start. The diversity of habitats in the region is revealed, including bogs, lochs and patches of ancient woodland, with a corresponding diversity of flora. A geology trail here illuminates the formation of the Assynt area, and part of the 'Moine Thrust' can be seen in the rocks of Knockan Cliff. There are excellent views from the top of the mountains of Coigach. Of these, Stac Pollaidh (2,008 feet/612m) is the most popular, and a relatively easy walk leads up from the minor road by Loch Lurgainn. Look for deer and birds of prey, and you may even see signs of wildcats. To the north on a clear day you can see the familiar form of Suilven (2,402 feet/732m), but this peak is strictly for experienced mountaineers.

There is a further extensive nature reserve at Inchnadamph. From this point the road leads round the shores of Loch Assynt, past the rocky ruins of Ardvreck Castle. Beyond this place is the popular harbour of Lochinver (this links up with a narrow and very scenic road from Loch Lurgainn). Up the coast, just north of the hamlet of Clachtoll, the circular remains of a broch from the first century AD can be seen on the shoreline.

Activity

WEST HIGHLAND LINE

Mallaig is the terminus of the West Highland Line, which is celebrated as one of Britain's most scenic railway routes. Its construction was no easy task – the peat bogs of Rannoch Moor were traversed with a floating bed of brushwood, beneath tons of ash and earth; the rocky heights of Glenfinnan and the deeply indented coastline had to be crossed. Contractor Robert MacAlpine pioneered the structural use of concrete, building the high viaducts which give such magnificent views. Sit on the left for the outward journey (reserve a seat at peak times).

LOCH NESS MAP REF NH4630

It would be difficult for anyone but the most hardened sceptic to gaze out over the waters of Loch Ness without just the small hope of seeing something which might be interpreted as a 'sighting'. Mentioned in writing as long ago as the 7th century, when St Adamnan's *Life of St Columba* tells of the saint calming the creature down after an apparent attack on a monk, the Loch Ness Monster – or, familiarly, Nessie – has become the focus of the tourist industry here. Drumnadrochit is the main centre for this, offering the Original Loch Ness Visitor Centre with a large-screen cinema, exhibition and sonar scanning cruises, and the Official Loch Ness Monster Exhibition with audio-visuals and a 'life-size' model of Nessie. You can hire a cabin cruiser, or visit the ruined Urquhart Castle on the shores of the loch, from where most sightings have been made.

Monster or no, Loch Ness is beautiful and it contains more water than all the lakes and reservoirs in England and in Wales put together. The loch is 24 miles (38.6km) long, 1 mile (1.6km) wide and 750 feet (228.6m) deep, making it one of the largest bodies of fresh water in Europe. The loch forms a major part of the Caledonian Canal, which links the west coast with the Moray Firth, and follows the line of the dramatic Great Glen, cutting Scotland in two halves. This spectacular geological fault has provided a way through the mountains for centuries of travellers and is tracked today by the A82 between Fort William and Inverness.

MALLAIG MAP REF NM6796

This small, busy fishing harbour, facing the Isle of Skye across the Sound of Sleat, stands at the end of the A830 from Fort William, more romantically known as the 'Road to the Isles'. The term comes from the cattle-droving days, before the railway arrived in 1901, but it holds the evocative promise of a special destination for today's travellers. It is also the last stop on the famous West Highland Line, and ferries from Mallaig can take you on to Skye, Rum, Eigg, Muck and Canna. The town has a heritage centre which illustrates the fishing industry of the town. The picturesque, old steam train *Jacobite* runs from Fort William to Mallaig, passing Morar on the way.

A couple of miles outside Mallaig, at Morar, the waters of Scotland's deepest freshwater loch tumble and cascade down a spectacular waterfall and into a beautiful sandy bay. One of the long, white-sand beaches along here provided the setting for the film Local Hero. A leisurely drive southwards is enchanting, passing through mixed woodland, with fine views to the islands. Allow yourself plenty of time – it's a slow, winding road and mainly single track until you reach the little church above Lochailort.

This part of the west coast has many associations with Bonnie Prince Charlie. It was at Loch Nan Uamh, south of Arisaig, that the Prince landed in 1745 to raise an army, and it was from here that he left for France after his defeat at Culloden the following year, leaving in his wake a strong tide of government retribution against the Highlanders.

Insight

MOUNTAIN MOGGIES

The hills of Torridon are home to many species, but the wildcats are among the most elusive. They live on the loneliest and most remote mountain sides, hunting at night for small animals and birds, though they have been known to take lambs and young deer. Pure-bred wildcats have litters in May, and are bigger than domestic cats, to which they are only distantly related. Their yellowy-grey fur is prominently striped in black, and they have thick, bushy tails. Around 24 inches (61cm) from nose to tail, they can be awesomely fierce, spitting and growling when roused, though they purr, like any cat, when contented. It is not always easy to recognise a pure wildcat, as so many have interbred with feral domestic cats.

SHIELDAIG & TORRIDON

MAP REF NG8154/NG9055

The villages around Loch Torridon are picturesque, but cannot compete with the grandeur of some of the finest mountain scenery in Scotland. The road east from Shieldaig, a whitewashed, 18th-century planned village overlooking the pine-clad Shieldaig Island, gives views over Upper Loch Torridon to the huge mountain mass dominated by what Queen Victoria called 'that extraordinary mountain, Ben Liathach.'

Of red Torridonian sandstone, 750 million years old and 3,360 feet (1,024m) high, Liathach has a row of seven peaks topped with shining white quartzite from 150 million years later. It forms part of the National Trust for Scotland's 16,100-acre (6,516ha) Torridon Estate. The Trust's Countryside Centre in Torridon village shows the best routes in the mountains, but guided walks are recommended if you want to tackle the 5-mile (8km) ridge between Liathach's peaks. The Deer Museum near by has a herd of wild deer, and information about their life on the hills.

Further on, Beinn Eighe presents a forbidding face to the traveller, but like the other mountains has impressive corries to the north. Britain's first National Nature Reserve was founded here in 1951 to protect the native Caledonian pine forest on its slopes.

The road north of Loch Torridon, with wonderful views over to the Applecross peninsula, passes through Fasag, built to house families displaced in the clearances, and through several crofting settlements to end at Lower Diabaig, from where you can walk to Redpoint, far out on the coast of Wester Ross.

CUILLIN HILLS ACROSS LOCH SCAVAIG

SKYE, ISLE OF MAP REF NG4844

Skye is the largest and most famous of the Inner Hebrides, dominated from every view by the high peaks of the Cuillins. The jagged gabbro (igneous rock, like basalt) of the Black Cuillins and the pink, scree-covered granite of the Red Cuillins have proved an irresistible challenge for mountaineers, and the most inaccessible peaks were only conquered at the end of the last century. To the north on the Trotternish peninsula is an extraordinary broken ridge from which peaks and pillars loom eerily on a misty day.

Road signs written in Gaelic as well as English quickly tell you that you're in a different culture, and Skye retains a strong Gaelic identity, encouraged at the college, Sabhal Mòr Ostaig, in Sleat. At the Aros Centre, just south of Portree, a forest walk illustrates the letters of the Gaelic alphabet. There are crofting museums at Colbost and Kilmuir, with reconstructed homesteads.

Portree is the island's capital, its colour-washed houses round the harbour, with fishing and pleasure vessels moored, are most attractive. This little town was named after a royal visit in 1540 by James V – port righ means king's harbour – and its formal square is a miniature delight. The town is the gateway to the Trotternish peninsula. Taking the road up the eastern side, look out for the distinctive column of the Old Man of Storr and other strange rock formations up on your left, and for the columnar formations and dramatic waterfall at the Kilt Rock on the coast to your right, just before Staffin. There are marvellous views from here across to the blue hills of the mainland.

Continuing around this peninsula you pass ruined Duntulm Castle and a memorial to Flora Macdonald, the Jacobite heroine who smuggled Bonnie Prince Charlie here from his hiding place in South Uist in 1746. The Prince, disguised as 'Betty Burke', continued his escape to Raasay and then on to France. Flora was arrested and briefly imprisoned in the Tower of London. She later married a Skye man and emigrated to America; they returned to live down the coast at Kingsborough, and Flora's grave is there.

Heading west from Portree brings you to the wilder side of the island, with the Waternish and Duinish peninsulas like two long fingers reaching out towards the Outer Hebrides. At Carbost, the Talisker Distillery produces a distinctive peaty, smoky malt whisky. Dunvegan is the family seat of another powerful Skye clan, the MacLeods, and claims to be Scotland's oldest inhabited castle, occupied since the 13th century. Surrounded by a stout wall, and heavily restored and harled in the mid-19th century, the castle is impressive if not beautiful – the treasures in its richly furnished rooms are well worth a look.

Broadford is the main centre for exploring the south of the island, and with its concentration of craftspeople, it is a good place to seek out good-quality souvenirs. The award-winning Serpentarium, run by experienced herpetologists, is well worth a visit. Here you can handle snakes, admire the

Sea Eagles at Portree Bay

A coastal walk to a raised beach called the Bile, returning by way of Ben Chracaig. While walking beside Portree Bay, keep at least one eye looking out to sea, you may spot the sea eagles that nest in the cliffs at Portree. The Aros Experience, just south of Portree, has the RSPB's closed-circuit TV link with the sea-eagle nest. Most nest action occurs between April and July (the young hatch in April), and the 'nest cams' give a magical insight into eagle chick behaviour as well as allowing people to witness the exact moment when a chick tentatively takes to the air for the first time.

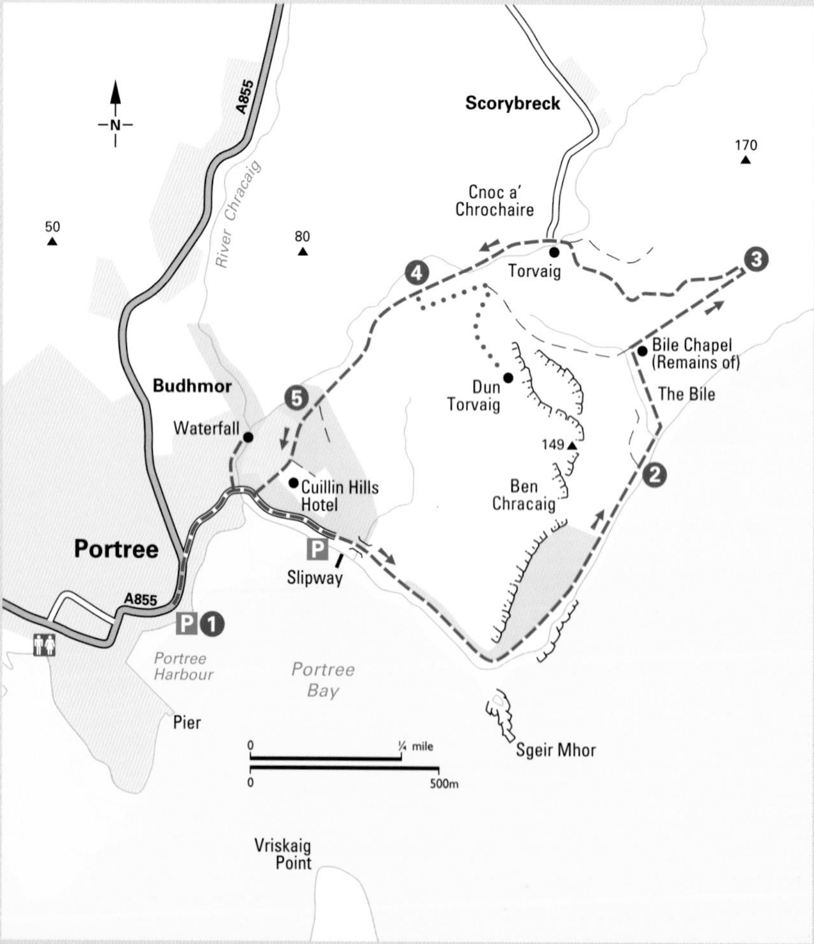

Route Directions

1 Turn off the main A855 on to a lane signed 'Budh Mor', to walk down to the shoreline and then continue to a small parking area. A tarred path continues along the shore past a slipway. After a footbridge, it passes under hazels which show the typical ground-branching habit of bushes formerly coppiced, cut back every seven years for firewood. The path passes below a viewpoint with flagpoles and then rounds the headland to reach the edge of a level green field called The Bile.

2 A wall runs up the edge of The Bile. A sign points up left for Scorybreck but ignore it and go through a small gate ahead. A rough path leads into the corner of The Bile field. Go up its left edge and turn across its top, to a stile just above a field gate. Cross the top of the next field on an old green path, to a stile at its corner. You will see a track just beyond.

3 Turn sharp left, up the track. At the top it passes through two gates to reach a stony road just to the right of Torvaig. Turn left past the house and cross the foot of a tarred road into a gently descending track. It runs down between two large corrugated sheds and then through to a gate with a stile.

4 The grassy path ahead leads down into Portree, but you can take a short, rather rough, diversion to Dun Torvaig (an ancient fortified hilltop) above. For the dun, turn left along the fence, and left again on a well-made path above. It leads to a kissing gate above the two sheds. Turn sharp right along the fence for a few steps, then bear left around the base of a small outcrop and head straight up on a tiny path to the dun. Remnants of dry-stone walling can be seen around the summit. Return to the well-made path, passing above Point 4 to join the wall on the right. The path leads down under goat willows into a wood where it splits; stay close to the wall.

5 At the first houses (The Parks Bungalow 5), keep downhill on a tarred street. On the left is the entrance to the Cuillin Hills Hotel. A few steps later, fork right on to a stony path. At the shore road, turn right across a stream and at once right again on a path that runs up for 60yds (55m) to a craggy little waterfall. Return to the shore road and turn right to the walk start.

Route facts

DISTANCE/TIME 3.5 miles (5.7km) 1h15

MAPS OS Explorer 409 Raasay, Rona & Scalpay or 410 Skye – Portree & Bracadale

START Portree on main A855 above harbour, grid ref: NG 485436

TRACKS Smooth, well-made paths, farm track, 3 stiles

GETTING TO THE START From the mainland, the A87 takes you to Portree. Follow the A855 into the town and then at the harbour take a lane down to the shore to find a small parking area.

THE PUB The Royal Hotel, Portree.
Tel: 01478 612525;
www.royal-hotelskye.com

lizards, frogs and tortoises, and learn more about their way of life.

If the weather is clear, drive over to Elgol to experience some of Britain's most magnificent scenery. The road winds below the mighty Red Cuillins and beside Loch Slapin before descending an alarmingly steep road into Elgol (not suitable for caravans). You can see across to the island of Soay, with Canna, Rum and Eigg to the south. Try to make time for a boat trip, which offers a dramatic glimpse of Loch Coruisk.

After the barrenness of the mountains, Sleat seems a veritable Garden of Eden. The lovely Armadale Castle Gardens and the Museum of the Isles is well worth a visit. There are excellent exhibitions about Clan Donald, genealogical research facilities, guided walks, a restaurant and much more. Look out for the special events held throughout the summer.

Skye is an unlikely crossroads among the islands. You can reach it by ferry from Mallaig (about 40 minutes), or across the strong currents by Glenelg (summer only), or across the new bridge at Kyle of Lochalsh. The bridge provoked controversy when it was built, but is low enough to be unobtrusive. Ferries to the outer islands leave from the harbour at Uig, on the Trotternish peninsula, and to Raasay from Sconser.

STRATHPEFFER

MAP REF NH4858

Once hailed as 'the Harrogate of the North', Strathpeffer is a curious phenomenon to find above the Highland line – a genteel, attractive little spa town, complete with Victorian architectural twirls such as verandahs and ornamental barge-boards.

Locals had known about the curative properties of the mineral springs here for centuries, but thanks to a serious scientific analysis of the water in 1819, Strathpeffer became a boom town. The first pump room opened the following year, and visitors flocked to fill the new hotels and villas. While never perhaps in the same league as Bath in Somerset, the town did attract some royal visitors from overseas, and the railway had to be specially extended from Dingwall to cater for the number of people drawn here. At the height of its fame there were even through-trains from London, though trains no longer come here.

Inevitably, tastes change, and Strathpeffer's popularity declined after the Second World War. Many of the spa buildings have disappeared, and the old wooden railway station now houses a museum of childhood. The Pump Room has been restored with interpretative displays covering the history of the spa. The town offers excellent golfing and recreational facilities to its visitors. Don't miss the Pictish stone slab, set in a field near the station. Deeply carved with an inverted, patterned horseshoe shape above a standing eagle, its original purpose is unknown.

There are several good places to walk here, including the ridge of Knock Farril to the south, and through the woods to the Falls of Rogie to the west. Salmon may be seen in the Blackwater River here, and there are pleasant picnic sites between the trees.

ULLAPOOL MAP REF NH1294

As you approach on the A835, the little whitewashed town of Ullapool is neatly laid out on a spit of land curving into Loch Broom. The tidy grid-plan of the streets reveals that this is a model town laid out to a plan developed by the British Fishery Society in 1788.

The site was chosen to provide a good fishing harbour, and to squeeze out the Dutch herring vessels which had taken advantage of the lack of local boats. The herring did not last, however, and, without the lifeline of the railway, the settlement declined.

The Fishery Society had chosen their site well, however, and in the first half of the 20th century boats came over from the east coast and fortunes revived. Until the mid-1990s, the local economy was given a boost by the 'Klondyker' factory ships from Eastern Europe, processing the catches of east coast trawlermen in the loch's sheltered waters. They went after the collapse of the Russian economy and now tourism is the main industry. Learn more about crofting, fishing and emigration at Ullapool's small museum, set in a former church.

Ullapool is the gateway to the remote northwestern tip of Scotland, as well as the main ferry port for Stornoway, in the Outer Hebrides. Around the coast at Achiltibuie is the Hydroponicum, a scientific delight, where bananas and other exotic plants thrive without soil – seeing is believing! At the head of Loch Broom, take time out to stop and see the dramatic Corrieshalloch Gorge, and the impressive suspension bridge just below the Falls of Measach.

Visit

THE SUMMER ISLES

This little group of islands lies just off the coast, some 12 miles (19.3km) northwest of Ullapool, and is well worth a visit if you enjoy peace and quiet – seals and seabirds are the chief inhabitants. Naturalist Fraser Darling lived on Tanera More and wrote his *Island Years* here. Today, fish-farming has replaced fish-curing as the main support for the islands.

Insight

A FAIRY TOKEN

A threadbare scrap of cloth, faded almost beyond recognition and displayed safely behind glass, is one of Scotland's best-loved talismans. This is the Fairy Flag of the MacLeods, supposedly presented to a clan chief, back in the mists of time, by his fairy lover, who promised that aid would be forthcoming if the cloth were waved in times of dire need. The flag has been used twice to turn the course of battle, apparently with great success, giving the lie to spoilsports who claim it is a banner stolen from Harold Hardrada in 1066.

Visit

OTTERS

Many people hope to see otters around the shores and lochs of Scotland, and, given a bit of luck, a good pair of binoculars and some local guidance, there is every chance you will. The Kylerhea Otter Sanctuary on Skye is a good place to spot these shy creatures. Loch Sunart on the southern coast of the Ardnamurchan peninsula, Loch Spelve in Mull and Loch Eynort in South Uist are good places where you may be able to see them. The Bright Water Visitor Centre at Kyleakin on Skye also has information about otters, and a museum to *Ring of Bright Water* author, Gavin Maxwell, who lived at the nearby lighthouse.

Strathpeffer and the Falls of Rogie

A fairly easy riverside and forest walk from the Victorian spa town of Strathpeffer to the Falls of Rogie. If you stand on the suspension bridge at the falls between July and September, when the river is fairly full, you might glimpse leaping salmon.

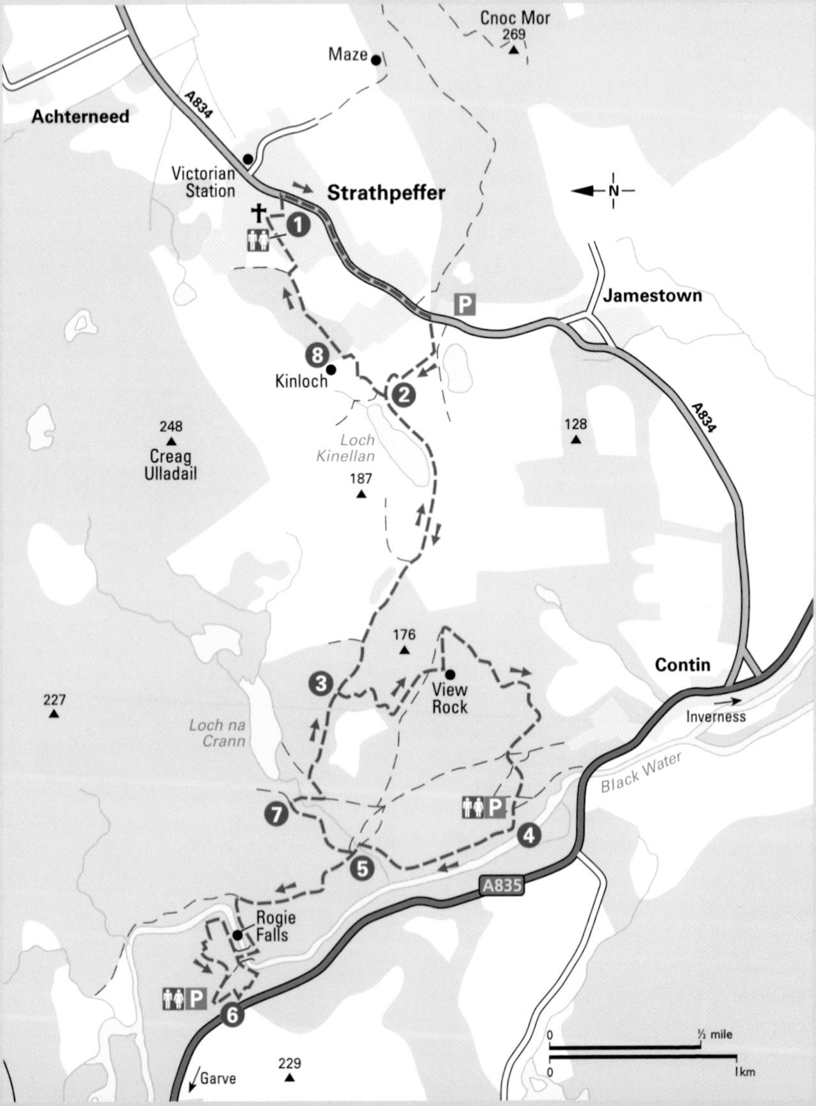

Route Directions

1 Head along the main road towards Contin. When you reach the edge of the town, turn right at a metal signpost for Garve then, at a bend in the lane, turn left, following another signpost.

2 Follow track to the left of Loch Kinellan. As it bends right, keep ahead up a path beside tall broom bushes to the corner of a plantation. Here you join a larger track leading into the forest. Continue for 0.5 mile (800m) until it reaches a signpost.

3 Turn left for View Rock on a good path with green waymarkers. At View Rock, a side-path diverts to the right for the viewpoint, then rejoins. After a long descent, ignore a green path off to the left and follow green waymarkers downhill. At a forest road go straight over beside a signpost. The path crosses two more forest roads to Contin Forest car park.

4 At the end of the car park, pick up a wide path, 'River Walk'. Where red waymarkers turn back right, keep ahead on a rougher path with deer head markers. It bends up right beside a stream to a forest road. Turn left, signed 'Garve', and in 80yds (73m) bear left, heading slightly downhill.

5 Go on for 600yds (549m), when a small track on the left is signed 'Rogie Falls Bridge'. At its foot, cross a spectacular footbridge below the falls and turn right, upstream. The path has green waymarkers and after 0.25 mile (400m) bends left, away from the river. It crosses rocky ground to a junction. Turn up right, to Rogie Falls car park.

6 Leave the car park through a wooden arch and follow green waymarkers back to the bridge. Retrace the outward route to Point 5 and turn sharp left up another forest road. It leads uphill to where a much fainter track crosses.

7 Turn right down the smaller track to pass between obstructing boulders, to a signpost. Turn left, signed 'Strathpeffer'. After 600yds (549m) it reaches the signpost at Point 3. Keep ahead and retrace the outward route to Point 2. Turn left on the tarred lane, which becomes a track. At Kinloch house bear right, then turn left through a kissing gate, with a second one beyond leading into a plantation with a signpost for Strathpeffer.

Route facts

DISTANCE/TIME 10 miles (16.1km) 5h

MAP OS Explorer 437 Ben Wyvis & Strathpeffer

START Strathpeffer, grid ref: NH 483582

TRACKS Waymarked paths and track, no stiles

GETTING TO THE START Strathpeffer lies on the A834 between Dingwall and Contin, 6 miles (9.7km) northwest of Inverness. Follow the main road into the town and find parking in the main square.

THE PUB Achilty Hotel, Contin. Tel: 01997 421355; www.achiltyhotel.co.uk

8 Follow the main path ahead until you see Strathpeffer down on the right. At the next junction bear right down the wood edge and turn right into town. The street on the left leads past a church with a square steeple, where you turn down right to the main square.

PLACES OF INTEREST

Aonach Mòr Gondola Ride
Torlundy.
Tel: 01397 705825;
www.nevisrange.co.uk

Armadale Castle Gardens and Museum of the Isles
Armadale, Sleat, Skye.
Tel: 01471 844305;
www.clandonald.com

Aros
Viewfield Road, Portree, Skye.
Tel: 01478 613649;
www.aros.co.uk

Beinn Eighe Visitor Centre
Aultroy.
Tel: 01445 760254;
www.snh.org.uk

Black Isle Brewery
Old Allengrange,
Munlochy, off A9.
Tel: 01463 811871;
www.blackislebrewery.com

Caledonian Canal Visitor Centre
Fort Augustus.
Tel: 01320 366493;
www.waterscape.com

Colbost Croft Museum
Colbost, by Dunvegan, Skye.
Tel: 01470 521296

Corrieshalloch Gorge National Nature Reserve (NTS)
Braemore.
Tel: 0844 493 2224

Cromarty Courthouse Museum
Church Street, Cromarty.
Tel: 01381 600418; www.cromarty-courthouse.org.uk

Dunvegan Castle
Skye.
Tel: 01470 521206;
www.dunvegancastle.com

Eilean Donan Castle
Loch Duich, Kintail.
Tel: 01599 555202;
www.eileandonancastle.com

Fortrose Cathedral (HS)
Cathedral Square, Fortrose.
Tel: 01667 460232

Gairloch Heritage Museum
Achtercairn, Gairloch.
Tel: 01445 712287;
www.gairlochheritagemuseum.org.uk

Glenfinnan Monument (NTS)
Glenfinnan.
Tel: 0844 493 2221

Groam House Museum
High Street,
Rosemarkie.
Tel: 01381 620961;
www.groamhouse.org.uk

Hugh Miller Museum & Birthplace Cottage (NTS)
Church Street, Cromarty.
Tel: 0844 493 2158

Hydroponicum
Achiltibuie, north of Ullapool.
Tel: 01854 622202;
www.thehydroponicum.com

Inverewe Garden (NTS)
Poolewe.
Tel: 0844 493 2225

Inverness Museum & Art Gallery
Castle Wynd, Inverness.
Tel: 01463 237114; www.invernesshighandmuseum.com

Loch Ness 2000: Official Loch Ness Monster Exhibition Centre
Drumnadrochit.
Tel: 01456 450573;
www.lochness.com

Mallaig Heritage Centre
Tel: 01687 462085;
www.mallaigheritage.org.uk

North West Highlands Geopark
Tel: 01571 844000; www.north-west-highlands-geopark.org.uk

Original Loch Ness Visitor Centre
Drumnadrochit.
Tel: 01456 450342;
www.lochness-hotel.com

St Andrews Cathedral
15 Ardross Street, Inverness.
Tel: 01463 233535

Skye Museum of Island Life
Kilmuir, north of Uig, Skye.
Tel: 01470 552206;
www.skyemuseum.co.uk

Talisker Distillery
Carbost, Skye.
Tel: 01478 614308;
www.scotchwhisky.net

Torridon Countryside Centre & Deer Museum (NTS)
The Mains, Achnasheen.
Tel: 0844 493 2229

Treasures of the Earth
Corpach, by Fort William.
Tel: 01397 772283; www.treasuresoftheearth.co.uk

Ullapool Museum and Visitor Centre
7–8 West Argyle Street,

Ullapool. Tel: 01854 612987; www.ullapoolmuseum.co.uk

Urquhart Castle (HS)
Drumnadrochit, Loch Ness. Tel: 01456 450551

West Highland Museum
Cameron Square, Fort William. Tel: 01397 702169; www.westhighlandmuseum.org.uk

FOR CHILDREN

Black Isle Wildlife Park
Drumsmittal, North Kessock. Tel: 01463 731656

Bright Water Visitor Centre
The Pier, Kyleakin, Skye. Tel: 01599 530040; www.eileanban.org

Highland Museum of Childhood
The Old Station, Strathpeffer. Tel: 01997 421031; www.highlandmuseumofchildhood.org.uk

***Jacobite* Steam Train**
Operates between Fort William and Mallaig. Tel: 0845 128 4681; www.westcoastrailways.co.uk

Kylerhea Otter Haven
Kylerhea, Skye. Tel: 01463 791575. Viewing hide.

Skye Serpentarium/ Reptile World
The Old Mill, Broadford, Skye. Tel: 01471 822209; www.skyeserpentarium.org.uk

Glendale Toy Museum
Holmisdale House, Glendale, Skye. Tel: 01470 511240; www.toy-museum.co.uk

SHOPPING

Castle Gallery
43 Castle Street, Inverness. Tel: 01463 729512; www.castlegallery.co.uk
Modern art.

Hebridean Jewellery
95 High Street, Fort William. Tel: 01397 702033; www.hebrideanjewellery.co.uk.
Jewellery in Celtic designs.

Highland House of Fraser Scottish Kiltmaker Visitor Centre
4–9 Huntly Street, Inverness. Tel: 01463 222789; www.highlandhouseoffraser.com

Highland Stoneware
North Road, Ullapool. Tel: 01854 612980; www.highlandstoneware.com

Highland Wineries
Moniack Castle, Kirkhill. Tel: 01463 831283; www.moniackcastle.co.uk

Holm Mills Shopping Village
Dores Road, Inverness. Tel: 01463 223311
Weaving exhibitions.

Inverness Farmers' Market
Eastgate Precinct, Inverness. Tel: 01309 651206

Nevisport
High Street, Fort William. Tel 0845 257 1344; www.nevisport.com
Outdoor adventure sports equipment and clothing.

Skye Batiks
The Green, Portree, Skye. Tel: 01478 613331; www.skyebatiks.com

Spean Bridge Mill
Spean Bridge, 10 miles (16km) north of Fort William. Tel: 01397 712260
Weaving mill.

SPORTS & ACTIVITIES

ADVENTURE SPORTS

Monster Activities
Great Glen Water Park, South Laggan, by Spean Bridge. Tel: 07710 540398; www.monsteractivities.com
Abseiling and archery to kayaking, windsurfing.

Raasay Outdoor Centre
Raasay House, Raasay, off north Skye. Tel: 01478 660266; www.raasay-house.co.uk
Sailing, cycling, climbing, kayaking and more.

Whitewave: Skye's Outdoor Centre
Kilmuir, Skye. Tel: 01470 542414; www.white-wave.co.uk
Rock climbing, kayaking, guided walks and more.

BOAT TRIPS

Bella Jane Boat Trips
Elgol, Skye. Tel: 0800 731 3089; www.bellajane.co.uk
Explore Loch Coruisk, the Small Isles and Skye wildlife.

Calum's Plockton Seal Trips
Shore Front, Plockton.
Tel: 01599 544306;
www.calums-sealtrips.com

Cruise Loch Ness
Knockburnie, Inchnacardoch, Fort Augustus.
Tel: 01320 366277;
www.cruiselochness.com

Dolphin Ecosse
Cromarty.
Tel: 01381 600323

Jacobite Cruises
Tomnahurich Bridge, Glenurquhart Road, Inverness.
Tel: 01463 233999;
www.jacobite.co.uk

Inverness Dolphin Cruises
Shore Street Quay, Inverness.
Tel: 01463 717900; www.inverness-dolphin-cruises.co.uk

Seaprobe Atlantis
Kyle of Lochalsh.
Tel: 0800 980 4846;
www.seaprobeatlantis.com
Glass-bottomed boat trips.

Summer Isles Cruises
From Achiltibuie.
Tel: 01854 622315

CYCLING

Barneys Bicycle Hire
35 Castle Street, Inverness.
Tel: 01463 232249

Island Cycles–Rod and Reel
The Green, Portree, Skye.
Tel: 01478 613121;
www.isbuc.co.uk
Cycle hire as well as fishing tackle hire.

GOLF

Fort Augustus Golf Club
Market Hill, Fort Augustus.
Tel: 01320 366660; www.fortaugustusgc.webeden.co.uk

Inverness Golf Club
Culcabock Road, Inverness.
Tel: 01463 239882;
www.invernessgolfclub.co.uk
18 holes.

Isle of Skye Golf Club
Sconser, Skye.
Tel: 01478 650414;
www.isleofskyegolfclub.co.uk
9-hole course.

Loch Ness Golf Course
Fairways, Castle Heather, Inverness.
Tel: 01463 713335;
9- and 18-hole courses; also leisure complex.

Strathpeffer Spa Golf Club
Golf Course Road, Strathpeffer.
Tel: 01997 421219;
strathpeffergolf.co.uk

LONG-DISTANCE PATH

Great Glen Way
Fort William to Inverness
73 miles (117km).
www.greatglenway.com

HORSE-RIDING

Gairloch Trekking Centre
Flowerdale Mains, Gairloch.
Tel: 01445 712652;
www.gairlochtrekkingcentre.co.uk

Highland Riding Centre
Borlum Farm, Drumnadrochit.
Tel: 01456 450220;
www.borlum.com

Highland Trekking and Trail Riding
Cougie, Cannich.
Tel: 01456 415323; www.highlandponytrekking.com

Skye Riding Centre
Suladale, by Portree, Skye.
Tel: 01470 582419; www.theisleofskyetrekkingcentre.co.uk

WINTER SPORTS

Nevis Range
Torlundy, north of Fort William.
Tel: 01397 705825;
www.nevisrange.co.uk
Ski and snowboarding centre for all abilities.

■ EVENTS & CUSTOMS

Gairloch
Highland Gathering, Jul

Inverness
Tattoo, Northern Meeting Park, late Jul

Plockton
Regatta, late Jul, early Aug

Portree
Skye Highland Games, Aug

Sleat
Skye Festival, Jun–Sep

Ullapool
Book Festival, May
Loopallu music festival, Sep

Tea Rooms

The Ceilidh Place

14 West Argyle Street, Ullapool, Highland IV26 2TY
Tel: 01854 612103

An Ullapool institution since it opened in 1970, this unique complex combines an all-day coffee shop, bar and a restaurant with a bookshop, art gallery and performance venue. Freshly baked cakes are part of the appeal of the all-day menu, but for something more substantial you might try the homity pie or Cullen skink, or perhaps a dish of locally caught fish. Dogs are only permitted in the garden.

Café Rhu

The Harbour, Arisaig PH39 4NH
Tel: 01687 450707
www.caferhu.com

Overlooking the bay at Arisaig, this popular and busy café is a gem. Home-made cakes and scones accompany morning coffee, tea or hot chocolate, and if you are sitting downstairs you can watch as lunches with an international gastro-twist are freshly prepared. Tuck into an aromatic lamb burger, a delicious bowl of Cullen skink soup, or perhaps a roll filled with black pudding. In the evening, special fine-dining menus make the best of local produce.

The Torridon

Torridon, by Achnasheen, Wester Ross IV22 2EY
Tel: 01445 791242; www.thetorridon.com

This Victorian shooting lodge on the shores of the loch is now a splendid country house hotel, offering the highest levels of service. High tea is a delight, offering sandwiches, fresh scones with jam and cream, and a selection of teas. By arrangement, they'll upgrade this standard, yummy treat to a champagne version.

Pubs

Applecross Inn

Shore Street, Applecross, Highland IV54 8LR
Tel: 01520 744262

Overlooking Skye and the Cuillins, this lovely traditional white-painted inn standing on the shore of the remote and lovely Applecross peninsula is known for its imaginative menu. Local fish and game appear on the menu, but it's the seafood that is usually outstanding, from the simplest prawn tails with Marie-Rose dip, to king scallops cooked in garlic butter with lemon, herbs and crispy bacon. Puddings are tempting too, with fruit crumble or raspberry cranachan on the list.

The Old Inn

Carbost, Isle of Skye IV47 8SR
Tel: 01478 640205

Stone walls and wooden floors characterise this former croft house, now an inn favoured by walkers and climbers. At one time rents were collected here. Now it serves traditional and hearty Scottish food, such as fresh mackerel, haggis and neeps, and baked salmon. The patio terrace overlooks Loch Hariport.

Plockton Inn and Seafood Restaurant

Innes Street, Plockton, Highland IV52 8TW
Tel: 01599 544222; www.plocktoninn.co.uk

Lying at the heart of pretty Plockton, this former manse is the relaxed and friendly setting for excellent food, whether you're looking for local langoustines, or maybe vegetarian haggis and clapshot (mashed potatoes and turnips). A smoke-house built behind the hotel adds to the variety of flavours on offer, and there are two gardens to enjoy in summer, or open fires in winter.

SCOTLAND TOURIST INFORMATION

VisitScotland
Level 3, Ocean Point 1, 94 Ocean Drive, Edinburgh EH6 6JH.
Tel: 0845 225 5121; www.visitscotland.com

Edinburgh & Scotland Information Centre
3 Princes Street, Edinburgh.
Tel: 0845 225 5121

Trossachs Discovery Centre & Aberfoyle Tourist Information Centre
Main Street, Aberfoyle.
Tel: 0845 225 5121

Inveraray
Front Street, Inveraray.
Tel: 0845 225 5121

Oban
Argyll Square, Oban.
Tel: 01631 563122;

OTHER INFORMATION

Historic Scotland
Longmore House, Salisbury Place, Edinburgh EH9 1SH.
Tel: 0131 668 8600; www.historic-scotland.gov.uk

National Trust for Scotland
Hermiston Quays, Edinburgh EH11 4DF.
Tel: 0844 493 2100; www.nts.org.uk

Scottish Natural Heritage
Great Glen House, Leachkin Road, Inverness IV3 8NW.
Tel: 01463 725077; www.snh.org.uk

Scottish Wildlife Trust
Cramond House, 3 Kirk Cramond, Edinburgh EH4 6HS.
Tel: 01131 312 7765; www.swt.org.uk

Royal Society for the Protection of Birds
Dunedin House, 25 Ravelston Terrace, Edinburgh EH4 3TP.
Tel: 0131 311 6500; www.rspb.org.uk

Forestry Commission Scotland
Silvan House, 231 Corstorphine Road, Edinburgh EH12 7AT.
Tel: 0845 367 3787; www.forestry.gov.uk/scotland

Cairngorms National Park Authority
14 The Square, Grantown-on-Spey PH26 3HG.
Tel: 01479 873535; www.cairngorms.co.uk

Traveline
Tel: 0871 200 2233; www.travelinescotland.com
For public transport inquiries.

Caledonian MacBrayne (CalMac)
Tel: 01475 650100; www.calmac.co.uk
Inter-island ferry operator.

Glenelg Ferry
www.skyeferry.co.uk

Royal Mail Postbusservice
Tel: 08457 740740; www.royalmail.com
Operates to inacccessible rural communities.

National Rail Enquiry Service
Tel: 08457 484950; www.nationalrail.co.uk
For all train enquiries.

ScotRail
Tel: 0845 601 5929; www.firstscotrail.com
Main rail services operator within Scotland; includes West Highland Line.

Scottish Citylink
Tel: 0870 550 5050; www.citylink.co.uk
Inter-city coach services.

Weather
www.accuweather.com

ORDNANCE SURVEY MAPS

A small selection of maps covering Scotland.

EDINBURGH & FIFE
Explorer 1:25,000; Sheet 349
Landranger 1:50,000: Sheet 66

TROSSACHS & SOUTHERN HIGHLANDS
Explorer 1:25,000; Sheet 365

ARGYLL, MULL & WESTERN HIGHLANDS
Explorer 1:25,000; Sheets 348, 358, 363

CAIRNGORMS & CENTRAL HIGHLANDS
Explorer 1:25,000; Sheets 401, 403

SKYE & NORTHERN HIGHLANDS
Explorer 1:25,000; Sheets 409, 410, 433, 434, 437

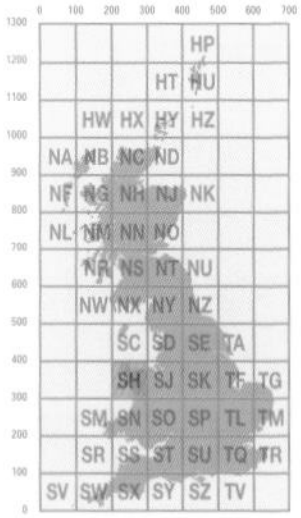

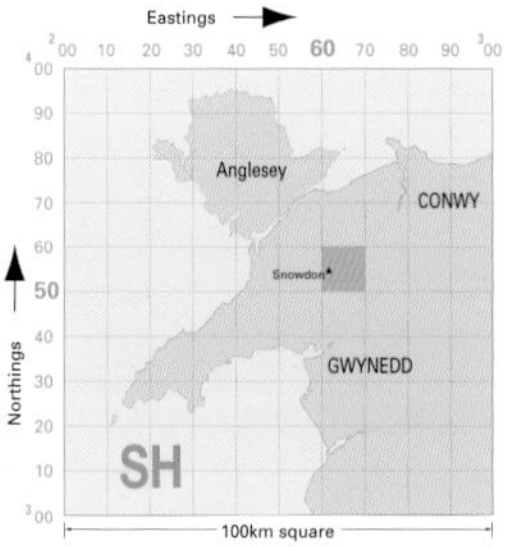

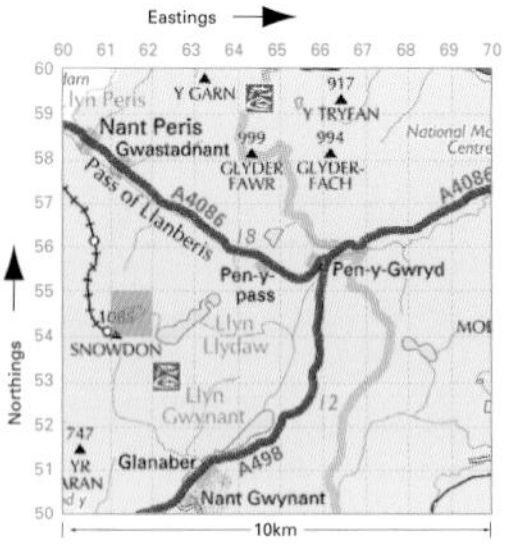

The National Grid system covers Great Britain with an imaginary network of grid squares. Each is 100km square in area and is given a unique alphabetic reference, as shown in the diagram above.

These squares are sub-divided into one hundred 10km squares, identified by vertical lines (eastings) and horizontal lines (northings). The reference for the square a feature is located within is made by adding the numbers of the two lines which cross in the bottom left corner of that square to the alphabetic reference (ignoring the small figures). The easting is quoted first. For example, SH6050.

For a 2-figure reference, the zeros are omitted, giving just SH65. In this book, we use 4-figure references, which allow us to pinpoint the feature more accurately by dividing the 10km square into one hundred 1km squares. These squares are not actually printed on the road atlas but are estimated by eye. The same process is carried out as before, giving an enhanced reference of SH6154.

Key to Atlas

M8	Motorway with number	B818	B road	Wick	Airport
	Motorway service area		Road tunnel	1343 Ben Nevis	Peak (height in metres)
5	Motorway junction with and without number	Toll	Toll		Built-up area
	Motorway under construction		Road under construction		National Scenic Area (Scotland)
A9	Primary route dual carriageway		Railway		National Park (England & Wales)
A85	Primary route single carriageway		Tourist railway	6	Walk start point
A8	Other A Road dual carriageway		National trail	1	Cycle start point
A74	Other A Road single carriageway		Ferry route	3	Tour start point
			County Boundary		
			National Boundary		

Cape Wrath
Durness
Kinlochbervie
Rhiconich
North-west Sutherland
Scourie
Eddrachillis Bay
Achfary
Drumbeg
Unapool
Clashnessie
Lochinver
Inchnadamph
Loch Assynt
Assynt - Coigach
Ben More Assynt
Loch Sionascaig
Knockan
Loch Lurgainn
Strathcanaird
Loch Shin
Shinness
Rosehall
Loch Hope
Ben Hope
Kyle of Tongue
Loch Eriboll
Loch Meadie
Altnaharra
Butt of Lewis
Port of Ness (Port Nis)
Cellar Head
Barvas (Barabhas)
Tolsta (Tolastadh)
Carloway (Carlabhagh)
Great Bernera
Lewis
Breasclete (Breascleit)
Miavaig (Miabhig)
Tiumpan Head
Stornoway
Stornoway (Steornabhagh)
The Minch
Balallan (Baile Ailein)
WESTERN ISLES
South Lewis, Harris & North Uist
Seaforth Island
Clisham
Tarbert (Tairbeart)
Scalpay
Harris
Leverburgh (An T-ob)
The Little Minch
Gruinard Bay
Laide
Cove
Aultbea
Loch Ewe
Melvaig
Inverasdale
Poolewe
Ullapool
Dundonnell
Loch na Sealga
An Teallach
Fionn Loch
Gairloch
Port Henderson
Loch Maree
Lochan Fada
Talladale
Beinn Dearg
Sgurr Mor
Loch Fannich
Ben Wyvis
Wester Ross
Kinlochewe
Lower Diabaig
Loch Torridon
Torridon
Liathach
Shieldaig
Garve
Loch Luichart
Achnasheen
Strathpeffer
Contin
Conon Bridge
Muir of Ord
Beauly
Kilmorack
Uig
Trotternish
Staffin
Loch Snizort
Lusta
Edinbane
Bernisdale
Colbost
Dunvegan
Portree
Sound of Raasay
Raasay
Rona
Inner Sound
Applecross
Bracadale
Skye
Drynoch
Carbost
Sconser
Scalpay
Kyle of Lochalsh
Balmacara
Kyleakin
Lochcarron
Stromeferry
Loch Monar
Glen Strathfarrar
Struy
Cannich
Drumnadrochit
Sgurr Na Lapaich
Loch Mullardoch
Loch Affric
Glen Affric
Sgurr Nan Gillean
The Cuillin Hills
Broadford
Sgurr Alasdair
Blaven
Torrin
Dornie
Inverinate
Glenelg
Shiel Bridge
Kintail
Sgurr Nan Ceathreamhnan
HIGHLAND
Invermoriston
Foyers
Whitebridge
Elgol
Soay
Isleornsay
Loch Hourn
Fort Augustus
Canna
Cuillin Sound
Sound of Sleat
Ardvasar
Ladhar Bheinn
Knoydart
Loch Cluanie
Loch Loyne
Great Glen Way
Invergarry
Loch Quoich
Loch Garry
Great Glen
Rùm
Mallaig
Loch Nevis
Loch Arkaig
Loch Lochy
Sound of Rum
Eigg
Sound of Eigg
Loch Morar
Arisaig
Loch Laggan
Gairlochy
Spean Bridge
Roy Bridge
Lochailort
Glenfinnan
Kinlocheil
Muck
Corpach
Eilean Shona
Loch Shiel
Fort William
Ben Nevis
West Highland Way
Loch Treig
Loch Ericht
Morar, Moidart & Ardnamurchan
Ardnamurchan Point
Acharacle
Salen
Kilchoan
Glenborrodale
Strontian
Ardgour
Onich
Kinlochleven
Blackwater Reservoir
Glencoe
Kentallen
Ballachulish
Rannoch Station
Coll
Tobermory
8
9
10
6

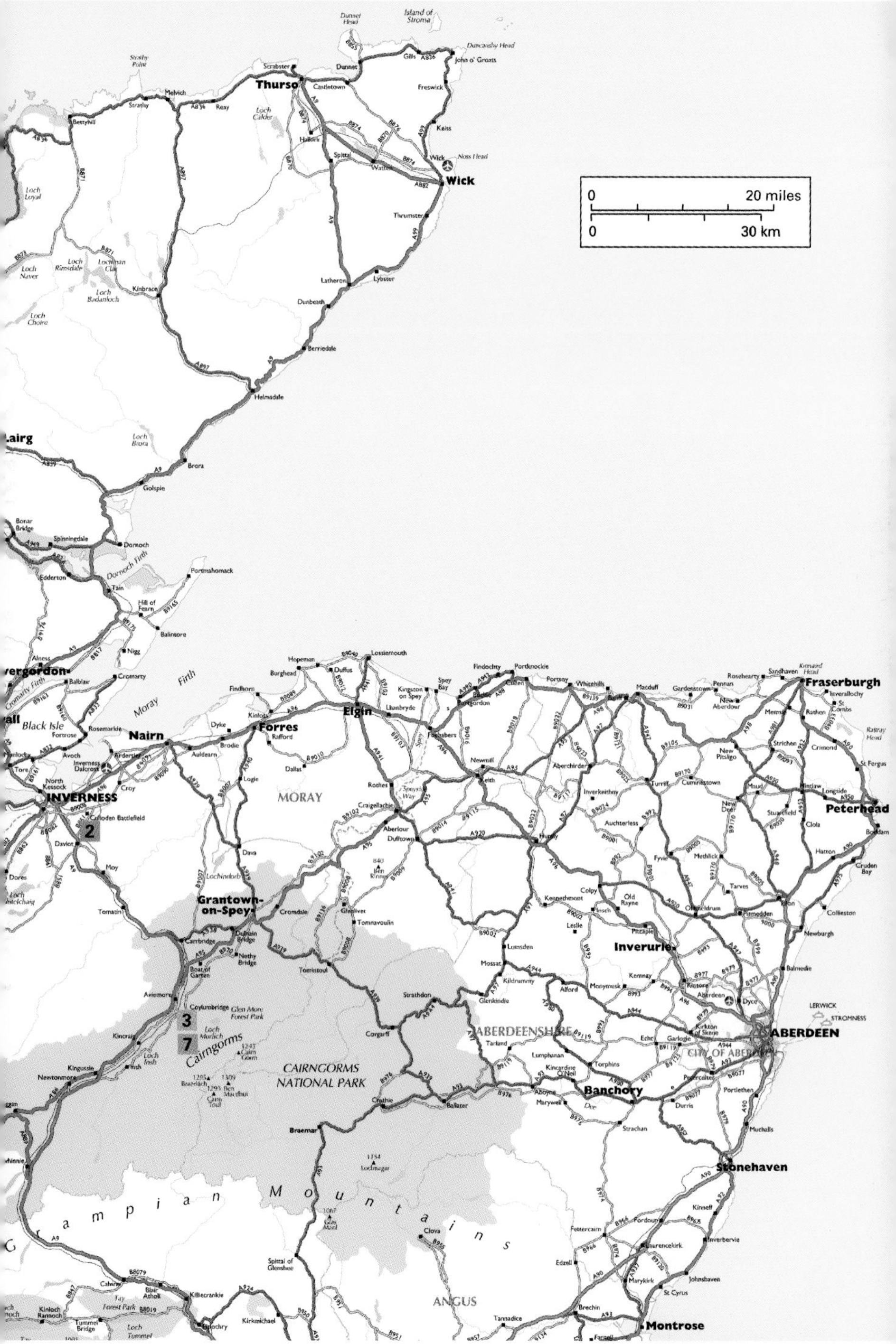

0 20 miles
0 30 km
Dunnet Head
Island of Stroma
Duncansby Head
John o' Groats
Gills
Dunnet
Scrabster
Thurso
Castletown
Strathy Point
Melvich
Strathy
Reay
Bettyhill
Loch Calder
Freswick
Keiss
Halkirk
Spittal
Watten
Wick
Noss Head
Loch Loyal
Thrumster
Loch Naver
Loch Rimsdale
Lochinan Clar
Loch Badanloch
Kinbrace
Loch Choire
Latheron
Lybster
Dunbeath
Berriedale
Helmsdale
Lairg
Loch Brora
Brora
Golspie
Bonar Bridge
Spinningdale
Dornoch
Dornoch Firth
Edderton
Portmahomack
Tain
Hill of Fearn
Balintore
Nigg
Alness
Invergordon
Cromarty Firth
Balblair
Cromarty
Moray Firth
Black Isle
Rosemarkie
Fortrose
Avoch
North Kessock
Tore
Inverness Dalcross
INVERNESS
Culloden Battlefield
Croy
Nairn
Ardersier
Auldearn
Dyke
Brodie
Findhorn
Kinloss
Forres
Rafford
Dallas
Burghead
Hopeman
Duffus
Lossiemouth
Elgin
Lhanbryde
Kingston on Spey
Spey Bay
Fochabers
Portgordon
Buckie
Findochty
Portknockie
Cullen
Portsoy
Whitehills
Banff
Macduff
Gardenstown
Pennan
New Aberdour
Rosehearty
Sandhaven
Kinnaird Head
Fraserburgh
Inverallochy
St Combs
Rathen
Memsie
Strichen
Crimond
Rattray Head
St Fergus
New Pitsligo
Mintlaw
Longside
Peterhead
Boddam
Maud
Stuartfield
Clola
New Deer
Cuminestown
Turriff
Aberchirder
Inverkeithny
Auchterless
Keith
Newmill
Rothes
Craigellachie
Aberlour
Dufftown
Huntly
Speyside Way
MORAY
Logie
Dava
Lochindorb
Daviot
Moy
Dores
Loch Ashie
Tomatin
Grantown-on-Spey
Cromdale
Glenlivet
Tomnavoulin
Ben Rinnes
Dulnain Bridge
Carrbridge
Nethy Bridge
Boat of Garten
Aviemore
Tomintoul
Coylumbridge
Glen More Forest Park
Loch Morlich
Cairngorms
Cairn Gorm
Kincraig
Loch Insh
Insh
Kingussie
Newtonmore
Braeriach
Ben Macdhui
Cairn Toul
CAIRNGORMS NATIONAL PARK
Corgarff
Strathdon
Glenkindie
Kildrummy
Mossat
Lumsden
Kennethmont
Insch
Leslie
Old Rayne
Colpy
Fyvie
Methlick
Tarves
Ellon
Hatton
Cruden Bay
Collieston
Oldmeldrum
Pitmedden
Newburgh
Pitcaple
Inverurie
Kemnay
Monymusk
Alford
Kintore
Aberdeen
Dyce
Balmedie
LERWICK
STROMNESS
ABERDEEN
CITY OF ABERDEEN
Kirkton of Skene
Echt
Garlogie
Peterculter
Portlethen
ABERDEENSHIRE
Tarland
Lumphanan
Kincardine O'Neil
Torphins
Aboyne
Banchory
Marywell
Dee
Durris
Strachan
Muchalls
Stonehaven
Crathie
Ballater
Braemar
Lochnagar
Glas Maol
Clova
Grampian Mountains
Spittal of Glenshee
Fettercairn
Fordoun
Kinneff
Inverbervie
Laurencekirk
Edzell
Marykirk
Johnshaven
St Cyrus
ANGUS
Brechin
Montrose
Tannadice
Kirkmichael
Killiecrankie
Blair Atholl
Calvine
Tay Forest Park
Kinloch Rannoch
Tummel Bridge
Loch Tummel
Pitlochry

Tobermory
Mull
Oban
Iona
Firth of Lorne
Loch na Keal, Isle of Mull
Sound of Mull
Ben Nevis & Glen Coe
LOCH LOMOND
& THE TROSSACHS
NATIONAL PARK
ARGYLL &
BUTE
STIRLING
Colonsay
Oronsay
Jura
Sound of Jura
Islay
Knapdale
Cowal
Dunoon
Helensburgh
Greenock
Dumbarton
Clydebank
Paisley
Largs
Bute
Sound of Bute
Kintyre
Arran
NORTH
AYRSHIRE
Ardrossan
Irvine
KILMARNOCK
Firth of Clyde
AYR
EAST
AYRSHIRE
SOUTH
AYRSHIRE
Campbeltown
Mull of Kintyre
Ailsa Craig
Girvan
Galloway
Forest Park
Newton
Stewart
Stranraer
Luce Bay
Wigtown
Bay
0
20 miles
0
30 km

Forfar
Arbroath
DUNDEE
PERTH &
KINROSS
PERTH
Crieff
St Andrews
FIFE
East Neuk
Fife Ness
Isle of May
Callander
STIRLING
CLACKMANNANSHIRE
Glenrothes
Kirkcaldy
DUNFERMLINE
Firth of Tay
Firth of Forth
North
Berwick
Dunbar
Falkirk
FALKIRK
Cumbernauld
Haddington
EDINBURGH
CITY OF
EDINBURGH
Livingston
WEST LOTHIAN
Dalkeith
EAST
LOTHIAN
Coatbridge
Penicuik
MIDLOTHIAN
Motherwell
NORTH
LANARKSHIRE
Berwick-
upon-Tweed
Holy
Island
Lanark
SOUTH
LANARKSHIRE
Galashiels
Kelso
Upper
Tweeddale
Pentland Hills
BORDERS
Southern
Upland
Way
Jedburgh
Hawick
Tweedsmuir
Hills
Lowther Hills
The
Cheviot
NORTHUMBERLAND
NATIONAL PARK
Moffat
DUMFRIES & GALLOWAY
NORTHUMBERLAND
Kielder
Water
Border
Forest Park
Pennine
Way
DUMFRIES
Castle
Douglas
Kirkcudbright
Solway Firth
CARLISLE
North
Pennines
DURHAM
NEWCASTLE
UPON TYNE
Morpeth
Alnwick
Wooler
Otterburn
Hexham
Alston
Langholm
Lockerbie
Annan
Gretna
Peebles
Selkirk
Melrose
Lauder
Duns
Coldstream
Eyemouth
Cockburnspath
Musselburgh
Leith
Kinross
Loch Leven
Dunkeld
Tay
Forest Park
Blairgowrie
Stirling
Dunblane
Doune
Kilsyth
M9
M8
M90
M80
M74
A74(M)
M6
A1
A7
A68
A69

The page numbers in bold refer to main entries.

The Automobile Association would like to thank the following photographers and companies for their assistance in the preparation of this book. Abbreviations for the picture credits are as follows – (t) top; (b) bottom; (c) centre; (l) left; (r) right; (AA) AA World Travel Library

1 AA/J Henderson; 4/5 AA/S Anderson; 8tl AA/R Weir; 8tr AA/R Elliot; 8c AA/S Anderson; 8b AA/S Day; 9 AA/S Whitehorne; 10t AA/S Day; 10c AA/J Henderson; 10b Dennis Hardley; 11tl AA/R Elliot; 11tr AA/S Day; 11cr AA/S Whitehorne; 11b AA/J Carnie; 13 AA/D W Robertson; 14 AA/J Henderson; 18 AA/D Corrance; 21t AA/K Blackwell; 21bl AA/K Paterson; 21br AA/S Day; 22c Phil Seale/Alamy; 22bl AA/J Smith; 22br AA/S Day; 23t AA/K Blackwell; 23c AA/J Smith; 23b AA/K Paterson; 38 AA/K Blackwell; 40 AA/J Smith; 43tl AA/S Day; 43tr AA/A Baker; 43b AA/S Day; 44tc AA/J Henderson; 44bl AA/J Smith; 44cr AA/S Day; 45t AA/K Paterson; 45c AA/J Smith; 45b AA/J Smith; 53 AA/S Anderson; 58 AA/D W Robertson; 65 AA/S Day; 66 AA/S Anderson; 69t AA/S Whitehorne; 69cl AA/S Anderson; 69cr AA/S Whitehorne; 69b AA/S Anderson; 70l AA/S Whitehorne; 70cr AA/S Anderson; 70br AA/S Anderson; 71t AA/S Day; 71c AA/R Elliot; 71b AA/S Anderson; 75 AA; 81 AA/S Anderson; 84 AA/S Day; 91 AA/S Anderson; 96 AA/M Hamblin; 99t AA/J Smith; 99b AA/J Smith; 100cl AA/J Smith; 100cr AA/J Smith; 100b AA/M Hamblin; 101t AA/R Weir; 101cl AA/R Weir; 101cr AA/R Weir; 101b AA/J Smith; 105 AA/J Smith; 111 AA/J Smith; 120 AA/A Baker; 122 AA/J Smith; 125tl AA/S Whitehorne; 125cl AA/K Paterson; 125tr AA/S Day; 125b AA/M Taylor; 126c AA/S Day; 126bl AA/J Beazley; 126br AA; 127t AA/J Carnie; 127c AA/J Carnie; 127b AA/J Beazley; 137 AA/S Whitehorne; 140 AA/S Whitehorne.

Every effort has been made to trace the copyright holders, and we apologise in advance for any accidental errors. We would be happy to apply the corrections in the following edition of this publication.